5/78 MIDWEST 13.94 7.398

Driving the Amish

Driving
the
Amish

Jim Butterfield

HERALD PRESS

Scottdale, Pennsylvania

Waterloo, Ontario

Library of Congress Cataloging-in-Publication Data
Butterfield, Jim, 1927-
     Driving the Amish / by Jim Butterfield.
        p. cm.
     ISBN 0-8361-9063-7 (alk. paper)
       1. Amish—Ohio—Holmes County—Social life and customs. 2. Farm
life—Ohio—Holmes County. 3. Amish—Ohio—Holmes County—Pictorial works.
4. Holmes County (Ohio)—Social life and customs. 5. Automobile travel—Ohio—Holmes
County. 6. Butterfield, Jim, 1927- . I. Title.
     F497.H74B87 1997
     977.1'64043'088287—dc21
                                 96-49840

The paper used in this publication is recycled and meets the minimum requirements of American National Standard for Information Sciences—Permanence of Paper for Printed Library Materials, ANSI Z39.48-1984.

All photos are by Doyle Yoder of Doyle Yoder Photography, PO Box 424, Berlin, OH 44610, and used with his permission. He offers a free catalog of books and publications, featuring America's Amish country.

Earlier versions of chapters were published in *Holmes County Traveler* (chaps. 4, 8, 11, 13, 14), *Northeast Ohio Avenues* (chaps. 10, 12), and *Pennsylvania Dutchman* or *Folklife* (chap. 9).

DRIVING THE AMISH
Copyright © 1997 by Herald Press, Scottdale, Pa. 15683
    Published simultaneously in Canada by Herald Press,
    Waterloo, Ont. N2L 6H7. All rights reserved except that Doyle Yoder
    holds rights to any other use of the photographs.
Library of Congress Catalog Number: 96-49840
International Standard Book Number: 0-8361-9063-7
Printed in the United States of America
Book design by Gwen M. Stamm/Cover photo by Doyle Yoder

06 05 04 03 02 01 00 99 98 97 10 9 8 7 6 5 4 3 2 1

To Dr. Alfred L. Shoemaker,
editor of the *Pennsylvania Dutchman* quarterly (now *Pennsylvania Folklife*),
who first encouraged me to write about the Ohio Amish.
Dr. Shoemaker was a founder of the Pennsylvania Dutch Folk Festival
at Kutztown, Pennsylvania, in 1950—
now the annual Kutztown Folk Festival.

Contents

Preface

THE Amish area around Holmes County has grown so large that plain families sometimes call van drivers or neighbors with cars to take them farther than horse and buggy can easily go. It is thirty miles north-south and east-west across the hills and valleys first settled by Ohio's Amish pioneers near Sugarcreek in 1808.

With my station wagon, I have been transporting plain people for some years. Driving through their slower-paced community now is a reminder of rural America's past.

In these stories, I am glad to share some experiences of driving for Amish folks. Most events in these chapters happened since 1990, when I retired from a factory job and began driving for Amish neighbors. Names of passengers are changed at their request, to protect their privacy and to support the high value they place on humility.

The Pennsylvania Deitsch (often called Dutch) spoken among themselves is a dialect of German. People who don't speak Deitsch are usually called *Englisch*.

Pennsylvania Dutch (or German) is a spoken folk language that does not have a standardized written form. *Budget* news scribes throwing in occasional Deitsch words might describe a dreary day as *drieb* or *dreeb,* and the word *day* itself might be spelled *Daag* or *Dawg.*

For the casual reader's sake, I spell Deitsch words phonetically to match their sound; as with *vee gehts* for "hello," *Haus* for "house," and *Froh* for "wife." A final *e* on Deitsch words is usually pronounced; as with *schaffe* (two syllables), "to work"; and *vare* (two syllables), "were." *Gut* (pronounced *goot*) is spelled with a *u* to look more German.

On the whole, the phonetic spelling system used for the dialect in the book follows English sound values rather than German sound values. This will make it easier for the reader who does not know German. I have also capitalized the nouns as in German. *Gut Gleek* (good luck) in picking up a little Pennsylvania Dutch as you read.

These reports are arranged in monthly or seasonal sequence to show a typical yearly pattern. The cycle of seasons and activities is brightly illustrated by Doyle Yoder's photographs.

Thanks to my patient wife, who encouraged me to set aside writing time and then became a work widow during the final weeks of completing chapters.

Gross Dank to all the local people who good-naturedly said it was okay to tell about their trips in my car.

Special thanks also to Abe E. Yoder and Isaac Keim, who checked out Pennsylvania Dutch phrases and quotations from the German Bible.

Verna Schlabach and Monroe Beachy at the Mennonite Information Center helped with wedding and income-tax details. Christian Schlabach and Mose A. Miller gave advice about ministers' duties.

Book editor S. David Garber was good at showing where to clarify events or add explanations for readers. Cecil Leslie of the Wayne County Writers Guild helped give some chapters better endings.

I hope you enjoy these trips into another world. In many ways, they show something of America's rural past. It is also the present for the Amish and their neighbors.

—*Jim Butterfield*

Auf dem Wege fragte er . . .

On the way he asked . . .
Mark 8:27

Driving the Amish

Stellet euch nicht
dieser Welt gleich.

Be not conformed
to this world.
Romans 12:2

1

Welcome

THE Weaver family was starting the New Year with a new baby. Little Erma came into this world on January third at 10:30 a.m., attended by the Weavers' family doctor at a rural birthing center near Mount Eaton, Ohio.

Jacob Weaver was a young farmer living about twenty miles away. His wife, Ada, was starting to hang laundry on a clothesline when she knew it was time to go. Jake left the pigs he was feeding and ran to the nearest telephone, at a pallet shop down the road. I'd been expecting his call to take them to the Mount Eaton Care Center.

Less than an hour later, Ada was "comfortable" in one of the birthing center's nine labor rooms. Each includes a little wooden crib for the infant and a brown-leather easy chair for the waiting father. Dr. Elton Lehman came in from his village office to see if Ada was making normal progress.

The modest Care Center was built in 1985 as Ohio's first free-standing birthing facility, not connected to a hospital. It was financed largely by Amish and Mennonite plain people living in and around Holmes County. They wanted a family-oriented birthing place without frills, insurance forms, or expensive equipment.

I noticed that two rooms were furnished with kerosene wall lamps for patients who prefer them to electric lights. Another room in the basement was labeled DRIVERS. It provides a resting spot for those who arrive at odd hours from more distant Amish settlements, like Ashland and Danville, bringing a pregnant woman about to deliver a baby.

About 450 babies are born at the Care Center every year. If a mother-to-be shows signs of complications, the Mount Eaton emergency squad quickly transfers her to a hospital in Orrville or Massillon, each twelve miles away but in different directions.

All went well for Ada and Jacob. When the time came, staff nurses brought a delivery table right into Ada's spacious room. Jake remained with his wife during the whole delivery. Then the staff brought a cot for him to use if he wanted to stay all night.

Erma weighed in at seven pounds, eight ounces. She roomed-in with her mother after Dr. Lehman and the nurse gave her the usual checkup and eye drops.

The birthing center allows families to be in the room with a happy mother and pleased father. So that first afternoon, baby Erma met two grandparents and the oldest of her five brothers and sisters.

In late afternoon Jake phoned me again for a ride home in time to milk ten cows. The grandparents, who live in a small *Dawdyhaus*, would help.

"Erma came too late to be another income-tax exemption for you," I kidded Jake as we drove along.

"I've already got all I need," he replied, "with the little we make on the farm."

"Big families are great when they can support themselves," I commented. "But is there always going to be enough food and jobs for everybody?"

"Well, I'll tell you," Jake countered, "there's plenty more room on the land for families if they'd live on small farms like we do. Some thousand-acre farms could keep ten families busy farming the way we do. The small farmer takes care of his land and tries to build it up. If there's a food shortage someday, it might be from overcropped soil on the big farms."

The next day quite a few relatives stopped in to see the newcomer. Some came by horse and buggy and tied up at a hitching rail behind the Care Center. I brought another set of grandparents from several miles south. Erma has lots of aunts and uncles, and dozens of cousins. Most of them will wait to visit her at home, but a few did come each day, sometimes sitting around the Care Center's lounge table to snack and talk.

That afternoon mother and child were ready for me to bring them home. Ada dressed her daughter in a white cotton undergarment and a pink flannel gown. She snugged a white knit cap onto Erma's head and tied it under her tiny chin. Wrapped in a blanket, the family's newest little dishwasher was ready to face the world. Jake paid most of the $350 bill for their two-day stay and said he'd be sending the rest next month.

"It sure is quieter here than at a hospital," Ada said as she came to the car. A nurse brought Erma while Jake carried personal belongings and supplies. The baby's face was veiled with a cloth to protect against the cold air.

"This is a good time of year to have a baby," Jake commented. "No garden work or canning right now."

"Well, that two yards of blue broadcloth I bought the day before coming here—," Ada reminded him. "Now you're going to have to wait till next month for a new work shirt. And I need to get a dress started for Erma, too, so maybe you'll have to wait longer."

"We'll all be taking orders from Erma for awhile," Jake chuckled.

When we pulled in the Weaver farm lane, three or four children watched earnestly for their new sister. Since their oldest child was only nine, Ada was glad to see a smiling neighbor—sixteen-year-old Amanda Miller—standing on the porch, ready to be their *Maud* (hired girl) for the next few weeks. It would be good just to sit quietly part of each day and nurse her new child.

"I also have to sew her a little white organdy cap for a head covering," the mother said as she moved toward the house, "before she goes along to church in about six weeks."

2

Old Christmas

"WE think this is the real Christmas," Fannie Hershberger said on January sixth.

She and her husband, Adam, were riding in my car to a family gathering near Charm, some twenty miles away. Old Christmas is an Amish holy day, observed by fasting till noon and not working except for necessary chores. This year it happened to fall on a Sunday.

"Church was about like usual," Adam said of their service that morning in a neighbor's house. "The ministers used Christmas texts from Luke and Matthew. One minister said there are different dates for Jesus' birth because the calendar was changed two or three hundred years ago.

"We had a gift exchange on December twenty-fifth, just like you," Fannie added, "except we don't have Christmas trees or Santa Claus. Then Old Christmas is more of a quiet day."

Quiet certainly described the village of Charm as we passed through. No stores or businesses were open. No one seemed to be out this cold, gray day.

"There's the school I walked to." Adam pointed toward a country one-room building farther on. "It was only a mile if we cut across the fields."

Adam's brother lives on the home farm, and that's where we pulled in. One long shed housed a buggy, a road cart, a pony cart, a spring wagon, and a two-seated surrey with brakes operated by a foot pedal. A banty rooster and two little hens scratched around the barnyard. A black collie barked, and a gasoline motor pumped water because no breeze was spinning the windmill.

When two school-age boys ran out to greet us, Adam caught one by the shoulders and swung him right off the ground.

"*Bischt gebuut von schaffe heit* (are you done in from working today)?" he kidded. Except for routine chores, no one really works on Sunday.

Another of Adam's brothers rattled in with a buggy, its horse looking warm despite the chilly weather. The bearded man hopped out to cover his mare with a big blanket and lift a hand-cranked ice-cream freezer from behind the seat. His wife climbed out, holding a plastic bowl of Jell-O. They went into the house with Adam for a conference about a sudden illness that had sent their father to the Millersburg hospital.

I sat in the car and read a weekly Sugarcreek *Budget* to see what was going on in Amish districts near and far. *The Budget* is Sugarcreek's newspaper, serving that town and other plain communities in North America. Aside from the weather, who's ailing, and who visited where, the following bits were sent in by scribes from Ohio, other states, and even Ontario, Canada.

Mt. Eaton, Ohio

Mt. Eaton district church was held at Roy A. Yoders'. Roys had supper and singing for the young folks, too.

Bonduel, Wisconsin

1995 ended with 34 households here,
200 people. Nine babies were born.
We have 16 dairymen, 9 carpenters, one
schoolteacher, one storekeeper, one
window manufacturer, and one raising
veal calves.

Guthrie, Kentucky

Ordination services were held in
N. District for minister . . . with the
chosen one in the lot being Daniel
Beachy. He is 39, married to Susie,
dau. of Amos Yoders, and they have 11
children.

Shipshewana, Indiana

Andy Masts were hit broadside by
a car. They escaped with only bumps
and bruises. The buggy was demolished.

After a while the two boys came out to start afternoon chores. They let me help feed four workhorses while they forked hay into their mangers.

"The big horses get one scoop each," a youth said as he showed me an oats bin, "and the two road horses each get half a scoop. Our pony here, Dusty, only gets hay because we don't use her much this time of year."

I helped them kick some fresh straw out into the heifer loafing shed, and we checked the hog feeders to be sure they still had chop in them.

"Now we have to feed our rabbits," said the younger boy as he led the way. Eight rabbits of different size and colors were in cages on the chicken house floor, so they could keep warm. The boys put rabbit pellets and water in each cage, gathered a few eggs from the hen nests, and spread mash in the chicken feeder.

Adam found us filling the water trough.

"My brother wants us to stay for supper," he said. "They're having homemade ice cream. What do you say we stay?"

The meal was buffet style—everything set on a corner table, waiting for us to help ourselves. First we stood for a few moments of silent prayer. Then everyone took a plate and loaded it with bread, wieners, ham slices, noodles, shredded-carrot Jell-O, tapioca pudding, home-canned peaches, and cookies.

We sat down around a larger table with a long bench behind it. Our host rolled in a tall floor lamp for light. The lamp was on casters to move easily. Its base was a tank of clear gas, and the light glowed from two mantles near the top.

"These are venison wieners," Adam's brother told us. "We had one deer made into bologna and one into wieners. We got about seventy pounds of meat from each one."

The deer had been right on the home farm. Ben had noticed them grazing in his field near the woods. On the first day of hunting season, he felled a buck for meat. He wants to keep some deer in the area, so he left two rows of corn standing unpicked over by the woods for this winter.

The ice cream was pecan, made from Knox Gelatin and real cream. Ice to cool the old-fashioned crank freezer was simply gathered from frozen puddles in the pasture.

After supper, brother Ben lit four lanterns to take to the barn for milking time. The family milks twelve cows—the parents four each, and the boys two apiece. They don't send milk out on Sunday, so by Monday morning there would be a dozen ten-gallon cans ready for the milk truck. It all goes to a Swiss cheese plant in the next county.

The family started for the barn, carrying warm water to wash the cows' udders, and we started the drive back to Adam's place.

"My dad isn't in good-enough shape to bring home," Adam explained. "It's his heart. We're going to take turns staying at the hospital till we see how much he improves. The best medicine right now is having us close by."

On the return trip, we drove past shadowy corn-fodder shocks in the dark fields. They looked like silent Indian encampments.

Occasionally we saw buggies on the road; they had had battery lights turned on or kerosene lanterns burning.

Adam works at a brickyard. There just aren't enough farms for the growing Amish population. A lot of men work at sawmills, feed mills, furniture shops, engine-repair shops, or small factories. Others go out with carpenter crews, masonry contractors, or house painters. Still others make harnesses, shoe horses, build buggies, or repair farm machinery.

When we got to his place back off the blacktop, Adam asked with a slight smile, "Do you know why I have such a long lane?"

I bit on that. "Why?"

"Because if it were shorter, it wouldn't reach out to the road!"

"Then you'd have to walk in to your house!"

"*Ya,* I guess so. Or your car would be stuck in the mud. But a horse could get through."

We all laughed at the friendly banter.

Since it was Sunday, and Old Christmas too, I didn't ask my riders for any pay that day. The Amish try not to transact business on the day of rest. They could pay me the usual fifty cents a mile later, or mail a check.

"*Shayna Grischtdaag* (nice Christmas)!" Fannie wished me as I turned the car around.

Next morning, in a history book at the public library, I learned that the Julian calendar of Roman times had a slight error that gradually moved spring—the vernal equinox—from March 21 to March 11. In the year 1582, Pope Gregory XIII corrected that by dropping ten days from the calendar.

Protestants were slow to adopt the change, but finally did after 1700. By then they were eleven days off. When the Amish ancestors had to skip eleven days, it seemed to them that January 6 of the Gregorian calendar came on the day that would have been December 25 on the old calendar.

That's why the Amish have Old Christmas on January 6. Other churches celebrate the same date as Epiphany, Three Kings' Day, or Twelfth Day, remembering the coming of the wise men to see the baby Jesus.

3

The Farm Sale

"Would you want to take me to that sale over by Trail?" Eli Miller asked one February morning. "I'd like to look at their pigs. I've got enough corn this year to feed a few more."

Eli farms 120 acres, and I'd seen him at other sales when his own work wasn't too pressing.

We started at about nine thirty, not rushing because livestock at farm auctions usually aren't sold till afternoon. The day was nippy, and ruts in Eli's lane were frozen hard enough to scrape the bottom of my car. Once on the good blacktop, I wondered out loud, "Shouldn't buggies have license plates to help pay highway costs?"

"We don't really need paved roads," Eli explained. "In fact, we have to weld borium on our horseshoes to keep them from slipping on pavement. Gravel roads would be plenty good enough for us. Why shouldn't the people who need paved roads pay for them?"

"Well, you do have kerosene and fertilizer delivered by truck."

"Yes, and we pay the truckers, too."

Then I asked, "Eli, what do you think about the U.S. government sending troops to Bosnia?"

"I'm glad I don't have to make that decision," he said. "We leave it up to government leaders, and we hope and pray they do the right thing. We support whatever the government says if it doesn't make us do something unchristian."

About the only farm work we noticed along the way was one horse-drawn manure spreader and a couple of men buzzing wood.

PUBLIC AUCTION signs guided us toward Trail, the crossroads where Holmes County's well-known bologna is made. Then we saw cars and trucks parked along the road, and buggies along a farm fence. The horses all had blankets tied over their backs on this chilly day. We had to walk the last eighth of a mile.

Near the barn, three men stood on a flatbed wagon. One in a cowboy hat chanted bids; the others held up small items and helped the auctioneer look for signals from the crowd.

"Sold at $20!" The auctioneer handed a good silage fork to a bearded bidder. The wagon was surrounded by men in denim jackets and black hats, with a number of *englisch* (non-Amish) farmers mixed in.

Next came three halters, a pony bridle, a tractor drive belt, two plow points, an old tarpaulin, a can of insecticide, several horse collars, and a small gasoline motor.

"All right, folks, here's a set of harness ready for your team," the cowboy announced in his quick pace. "Who'll say $200? $100? $75? Yes, I've got $75 —now $100? Yes, $150? Got $150, now $200? Got $200, now $250? Yes, now $300? Now $350? Now $375? Got $350, who'll say $375? $360 anybody? Sold right there for $350!"

Then the crowd moved out beyond the barn to a row of typical horse-drawn implements. The sun started warming the ground, and one fellow said approvingly, "*Shayna Daag* (nice day)."

The farmer selling out was still a young man, about thirty years old, with a wife and four children. He'd been renting the land as a good way to start farming without a huge mortgage. Then the owner wanted to sell, but the house and other buildings were quite old. The young family decided that if they sold their cattle and equipment, they'd have enough to build themselves a nice new house, and the husband could go to work on a carpenter crew.

"All right, let's start with this spring-tooth harrow," the auctioneer began. "This is a $100 harrow if I ever saw one. Who'll give that? $100? Yes, there's the hundred. Yes, now $125? Yes—now $150? Yes, $175? $160 then? Yes, got $160, need $165. $165? . . . Sold at $160!"

The crowd moved from one implement to the next with spirited bidding on a cultivator, a plow, a hay rake, manure spreader, grain binder, corn sheller, field disc, and box wagon. A field mower sold for $350.

There are disappointments at every sale, and this time it was a sound Farmall tractor on solid rubber tires. It was the type of tractor used for threshing, filling silo, and shredding corn fodder. It only brought $1,875. "Somebody send for the sheriff," the auctioneer groaned. "This was a real steal!"

By that time a lunch line was forming at the house. Divided trays were stacked inside the kitchen door, and women in plain dresses and aprons were serving up a sale menu:

Chili	.65
Chicken noodle soup	.55
Sloppy joe	1.25
Ham & cheese	1.25
Coney dog	1.00
Jell-O	.25
Hot chocolate	.25
Coffee	.25
Pie	.65

    cherry
    apple
    banana cream

It felt good to pass through the warm kitchen and choose some hot food. The girl who took our money was wearing a white cap and punching a battery calculator to add up totals. We sat on benches in the next room, and I asked an *englisch* (non-Amish) couple if they had come to buy livestock.

"A cow," the wife replied. "But there probably won't be any bargains.

There must be three hundred people here, and there are only eleven cows."

I listened for more talk about former Yugoslavia but only heard local chitchat. On my way out the side door, I quizzed a plain-dressed man, "What do you think about what's happening in Bosnia?"

"Our bishop said there'll be one last war sometime," he answered. "The main thing is to be sure we're ready for God's final judgment. It says in Revelation that blood will flow as high as a horse's mouth."

After lunch pigs were being sold, and my passenger, Eli, was trying to get at least six. However, most pigs were small and were still with their mothers. The sows were being sold with their suckling pigs for big figures: $350 for one with nine pigs, and $375 for one with eleven piglets.

Finally Eli had a chance at weaned feeder pigs and bid some up to $35. Someone else got them for $40.

"I'm ready to go home," he decided.

We hung around long enough to see some cows sell for $800. The best workhorse went for $1,300.

The couple I met at lunch who wanted another cow did go ahead and pay $950 for a five-year-old holstein that was producing sixty-five pounds a day. They were nudged to that bid by the auctioneer who coaxed, "It's not what you pay—it's what you take with you."

When we left, the midafternoon sun had softened the ground, and young boys in boots were having fun slopping around in the surface mud.

Eli asked, "Is it okay if another man rides partway back with us?"

"Fine," I replied.

On the way I drew out the new passenger's opinion on the current news. "What do you think about sending troops to Bosnia?"

"Maybe somebody has to stop people from killing each other," the older man said. "We Amish can't do anything about it—we won't fight, you know. Jesus said, 'Love your enemies.' And he didn't fight or let his disciples fight. He came to save, not to destroy. During the Second World War, many of us served in camps for conscientious objectors. We're willing to do constructive things, even dangerous service. I was a firefighter out in Montana."

We let him off at a side road and soon passed wagons going home from the sale. One had chickens in a crate. Another carried ten-gallon milk cans banging together. We figured all cow buyers would have to move their new animals by nightfall.

"An auction like this—selling livestock and implements but not the land—might add up to $45,000 or $50,000," Eli guessed.

It had been ten miles one way to the auction. I asked Eli, "How long would such a trip take by horse and buggy?"

"Most of an hour," he guessed. "This is good traveling weather for horses, but I don't like to leave mine standing so long in the cold. And my church doesn't use storm fronts on buggies," he added. "So a long trip gets to be a little cool for me, too."

At Eli's lane, he rolled down the car window to check their mailbox. He got a seed catalog, a farm magazine, a milk check, a feed bill, and a letter from his son who lived near Nappanee, Indiana.

"I'll see what pigs bring at the Mt. Hope auction next week," Eli said. "You know how we are about sales—it's the only excuse we have to get out of work for the day!"

4

A Wedding

"ARE you nervous?" I asked Katie Yoder at noon the day before she was going to be married.

"Not yet," the nineteen-year-old replied as she got into my car that February day.

Katie was making a quick trip to the grocery for a few items her mother needed to prepare the wedding dinner.

Often they go six miles by horse and buggy to shop, but time was running short, so they asked me to drive. Katie went because her mother was busy cutting up chicken and baking pies for the big event on Thursday. Several neighbor women were in the kitchen, too, making dressing, blending pudding, and stirring Jell-O for two hundred guests.

"We got seventy broilers from Gerber Poultry in Kidron," Katie told me on the way. "We washed up about a hundred pounds of our own potatoes to cook tomorrow morning. And we're baking thirty-three pies today."

I soon parked at the supermarket, and Katie hustled through the aisles—a slim figure in black bonnet and shawl, pushing one of the shiny carts. She checked out with eight boxes of crackers, several pounds of butter, three hands of bananas, a box of book matches, and toothpicks.

On the drive back, Katie described her wedding dress. "It's dark blue. I made it a month ago already. The waitresses are going to wear dusty blue. They only had three weeks to make their dresses."

Amish couples planning to marry keep it secret until their intentions are announced in church just three or four Sundays before the event.

Katie is the third of fourteen children and has one married sister. She had helped her mother with the endless washing, cooking, cleaning, sewing, gardening, canning, and childcare. She had also milked cows, fed chickens, husked corn, canned beef, washed buggies, and begun to quilt.

Besides that, she likes to read and had gone through most of James Herriot's series about animals that started with *All Creatures Great and Small*.

Dan Troyer—the young fellow Katie will marry—was also only nineteen. Neighbors remarked at how young they were, because most Amish youths wait until they are of age, twenty-one. Children usually work for their parents until they are twenty-one. If underage children work away from home, their wages often go to the parents.

Dan has a good job at a cabinet shop. It's fine if he prefers woodworking, because he has eight other brothers and sisters still on the home farm.

When we got back with the groceries, Dan had just brought a wagonload of church benches and was unhitching the team of horses. He was staying at the bride's home to help set up for the wedding dinner there and the ceremony nearby.

* * *

The big day started for them, ready or not, with buggies and surreys coming in the lane before eight o'clock. Three hostlers, picked by the bride and groom, helped families unhitch and put their horses in two barns.

The service and the wedding ceremony was in a neighbor's large workshop. It lasted from eight thirty to noon, with much singing and preaching on Bible references to marriage. Dan and Katie and four attendants sat on chairs in the center, facing each other, with women on benches behind the bride and men on benches behind the groom.

During one of the long slow tunes, the young couple followed all the ministers present to a separate room. There the bishop offered half an hour of serious counsel. The next day, the bishop told me some of the advice he gave.

"Start your married life with a prayer," the bishop instructed, "and then let prayer be a daily occasion. Set aside a time for devotions together every day.

"Marriage is not so much a physical union as a spiritual bonding."

Whether they needed it or not, he reviewed some facts of life, including a reminder to the man to be considerate of his wife's physical nature.

Again the bishop stressed, "Marriage is permanent." He asked the couple, "Are you certain you are ready to remain lifelong companions?"

"*Ya,*" they replied.

Back with the assembled guests, after all the preaching and Scripture reading, the bishop invited Daniel and Katie to stand before him.

He addressed the couple, "Do you acknowledge that it is right for one man to have one wife?"

"*Ya,*" they answered.

The bishop asked Daniel, "Do you think the Lord has provided this sister-in-the-faith to be your wife?"

"*Ya,*" he answered.

The bishop asked Katie, "Do you think the Lord has provided this brother to be your husband?"

"*Ya,*" she answered.

Next he asked Daniel, "If your wife becomes ill, will you care for her as a Christian husband should?"

"*Ya.*"

He asked the same of Katie. "If your husband becomes ill, will you care for him as a Christian wife should?"

"*Ya.*"

To the couple, he inquired, "Do you promise to live together until the Lord parts you?"

"*Ya.*"

"*Ya.*"

That covenant was followed by prayer.

Quoting from Tobit (in the Apocrypha), the bishop took Katie's right hand, placed it in Daniel's hand, and pressed them together with his own.

"*Der Gott Abrahams, Isaaks, und Jakobs, sei mit euch und helfe euch zuzammen und gebe seinen Segen reichlich über euch, und das alles durch Jesus Christum. Amen.* (The God of Abraham, Isaac, and Jacob be with you together and help you and give his rich blessing upon you, and this all through Jesus Christ. Amen)."

There was no ring and no kiss. The Amish do not wear jewelry. They are reserved in public and prefer not to show affection in front of others.

"You are now man and wife," the bishop said, "and cannot part from each other without death or great sin."

During most of this long service, Katie's mother had stayed at home, directing the cooks and getting everything ready for dinner. But at about eleven thirty, she and other kitchen helpers walked over to the neighbor's shop in time to witness the promises made and the joining of hands.

* * *

The happy throng headed back to the bride's farm for chicken and all the trimmings. With their four attendants, the new Mr. and Mrs. Troyer sat in the *Eck*, the corner of arranged tables. They found a three-tier cake before them, and tall glass bowls of mixed fruit. Hand-painted plates marked each couple's place.

Guests seated themselves on benches at long tables stretched end to end in every room. When all the benches were full, everyone bowed their heads reverently for silent grace.

Then the young women in dusty blue brought pan-baked chicken, heaps of mashed potatoes, dressing and gravy, lettuce salad, platters of cheese and bologna, loaves of bread and spreads (peanut butter and honey, apple butter, jelly), bowls of fruit, date pudding, frosted cake, two kinds of pie, and ice cream!

After dinner, the newlyweds opened presents: tools, kitchenware, china sets, bedding, lamps, chairs, food—a huge pile of useful things that would fill a wagon. And a wagon was just what they needed. The day after tomorrow they planned to move to a basement home and set up housekeeping.

Why day *after* tomorrow? Because on the first day after the wedding, the new couple and their four attendants would wash all the wedding party dishes, scrub all the borrowed pots and pans, and clean the mother's hopelessly snarled kitchen.

Fortunately, they would surely get some good-natured help from various joking brothers and sisters or from a few cousins and friends who would stop by to wish them God's blessing.

5

Income Tax?

NOAH ZOOK noticed that a local hospital was going to offer health screening tests for seniors and asked if I could take him there. I signed up for the public service, too, and picked him up at his crossroads village home. Someone was tapping sugar maple trees right along the main street that March day.

"I hear spring coming," Noah said as we listened to sap plunking into new pails hanging on several tree trunks.

Driving to the hospital, we passed a farm he had rented on shares back in 1955, and our talk naturally turned to his farming experience.

"For eight years I rented for half the crops," Noah told me. "I owned the cows and got the whole milk check. When my wife and I milked ten cows, we usually sent five cans a day to the cheese factory.

"That was when our children were small. By 1960 we had $5,000 saved to put down on a farm of our own. Our oldest boy was thirteen by then, ready to help handle eighty acres. Our girls were big enough to milk cows, so we increased our herd to fourteen. An average monthly milk check was $600.

"Our new farm cost only $25,000—before property went sky-high." Noah rolled his eyes. "But a $20,000 debt seemed like a lot. We bought five hundred straight-run chicks. That means half of them were roosters, which we ate or sold. Then egg money from the hens almost paid our grocery bill.

"We usually had five or six sows and fattened their litters; but if pigs were high, we sold them. We tried to raise all our own hay and straw. A farmer can bring a lot of weed seeds in if he gets bales from somewhere else.

"One of our first projects was to fight the weeds. Three of the children and I went through the fields with empty fertilizer bags. We pulled and carried off all the wild mustard we saw. It took us more than half a day. After doing that every spring for twenty years, I did it myself in two hours one spring.

"Another thing that paid off," Noah went on, "was clearing the fencerows and putting good woven-wire fence around the pasture. That gave us lots of wood to burn from the trees we cut. It let me plow right to the edge of fields, without shade on the crops.

"We kept all our heifer calves and sold the bull calves. I did keep a bull sire all the time, till he was three or four years old, or got too mean. I could sell a big, heavy bull for a lot more than it cost to buy a lighter young one."

"So," I asked, "did you ever end the year owing income tax?"

"No," Noah replied, "not till the children were of age. My gross most years was about $25,000, but my net was around $8,000."

I almost steered off the road. "What? $8,000! How did you pay for a whole farm on $8,000 a year?"

"Well, I sold off $6,000 worth of timber and still had enough lumber for a new barn," Noah recalled. "But I made the biggest gain when my boys went out to work. Aden started working at the pallet shop when he was sixteen. That brought in $5,000 toward reducing the mortgage.

"At eighteen, Aden went for alternate service as a hospital orderly during the Vietnam War. He was only paid $1.70 an hour, but that meant $3,000 a year extra for us at the very time the next son, Ivan, was also earning $5,000 as a teenage nailer at the pallet mill. All that helped whittle down our mortgage ahead of schedule.

"We were out of debt in twelve years." Noah smiled as we parked for our physical exams.

We joined a line of men, filled out forms, had blood samples taken, and waited for the volunteer doctors to check each person.

"When our sons came of age, at twenty-one, and were going to get married," Noah explained, "we gave them livestock and furniture and quilts."

The hospital staff said the results of our physicals would come by mail, so we headed back toward the sap buckets.

"Another way I got ahead," Noah continued, "was by never hiring help. Instead, I worked out some myself. One winter I butchered nine beefs for other people. And I did some smaller carpenter jobs. Of course, we had our own eggs, milk, meat, and garden vegetables, in season and canned. And my wife made our clothes.

"I bought most of my farm equipment at sales and raised some replacement horses at home. My buggy cost $600 and lasted for over twenty years.

"Real-estate tax was the biggest bite," Noah groaned. "About $860 a year. I figure I worked one whole month just to pay that.

"By rotating crops and spreading manure, we watched our soil improve and the yields increase.

"When I planted silage corn, I put soybeans in the pea hopper with the corn, the type that would climb up the stalks, and sorghum seed in with the fertilizer. That way I grew sweet protein with the cornstalks. With all that chopped up in the silo, I didn't have to buy as much dairy supplement for my cows."

Noah also had another way to get the most nutrition out of corn. "I didn't leave it standing in the field to be husked by hand. As soon as the ears were dented and ripe enough, I cut and shocked the stalks while they were still green and sappy. The ears dried in the shock, but the stalks still had a lot more feed value than if they were left to turn brown in the row.

"When I had my own husker," he said referring to the noisy rig that looks like a small threshing machine, "I could husk four loads of corn shocks by myself while the children were in school. That would fill two box wagons with ear corn and give me fresh fodder to feed the cows and horses. What the animals didn't eat went down under their feet and made good bedding. I saved a lot of hay and straw that way.

"Corn borers can live in cornstalks over winter in the field," Noah explained about a bothersome insect. "But they won't live in stalks that go through manure in the barn. So I think there are good reasons to use up the corn fodder in the barn. Whenever our fodder was gone, the cows wouldn't give as much milk," he observed. "Besides, I didn't have to do all that husking out in the field by hand!"

That was as much farming advice as I could absorb in one day, so I shifted the subject. "When did you quit farming? How much did your farm sell for?"

"That's when a farmer finally gets his pay," Noah remarked, "when he sells out and settles up. I had bought the woods behind our place, so that made the farm 117 acres. It brought $123,000 in 1977."

Just then we came to a shed labeled ROY'S WOODWORKING, with **Income Tax Service** lettered lower on the sign.

"Let's stop here a minute," Noah requested. "Since I got into selling wood crates from my shop, it seems like I always owe something. Right now I'm making a hundred cantaloupe crates for a produce grower at the edge of town."

He picked up forms and made an appointment for help with tax reporting.

I asked Roy, "Out of a hundred farmers using horses, how many actually pay some income tax?"

"In my experience, I'd say five or ten," he stated. "So far this year, the Amish farm gross has varied from $25,000 to $75,000. An average family might have a net of $20,000. With six or eight children, they wouldn't owe anything."

As we reached Noah's village home, he said, "It was hard to leave the farm. I would have just stayed there if any of my children had wanted it. But Aden already had a farm of his own. The younger boys were making furniture, and one of them had started a stove-and-lamp business."

"Well, how many grandchildren do you have by now, anyhow?"

Noah smiled as he tallied his true treasure. "Thirty grandchildren, and five great-grandchildren!"

He stepped over to the closest sap bucket and looked in.

"A couple inches already." He held up two fingers. "Makes me want to start spading the garden."

During his twenty-five years as a tiller of the soil, Noah always got up by five in the morning.

"Farming pays well," he commented in parting, "if you don't count all the hours you put in!"

6
The Barn Raising

Mrs. Jonas Schlabach sent a letter asking if I could take her to a massage therapist in Berlin. She had stiff shoulders and neck pains that made cooking uncomfortable. Dishwashing and laundry was even more painful. She had nine sons and no daughters, so there wasn't much help around the house.

By eight o'clock on Friday morning, I was driving downslope toward her farm. Suddenly, at the crossroad before her place, there was Mahlon Mast's barn in smoldering ruins! Knots of neighbors were standing around to stare at the charred loss. Smoke was still curling up from hot piles where grain bins had stood.

"The fire started before chore time," Mrs. Schlabach told me when I got to her house. "Fortunately, someone was up before daylight and saw the flames. They got all the horses out while the barn was burning above, and a neighbor let the cows out into pasture. The fire started inside, by an open door near the road, so they think somebody set the blaze."

An *englisch* farmer up the road saw flames so bright that at first he thought one of his own buildings was on fire. His wife called the Apple Creek Volunteer Fire Department while he rushed over in his pickup and helped Mahlon pull some machinery out through the big front doors.

"The fire was so bright," Mrs. Schlabach said, "that our roosters started crowing. The fire trucks couldn't do anything except wet down some other sheds and the silo. The barn burned so fast that the last fire truck left by seven o'clock."

On the way to Berlin we discussed other suspicious fires that had plagued the area. Two full barns not two miles away were probably set by arsonists. Then a smaller barn burned with the family's favorite horse still in it. Just a few weeks earlier, Mahlon had heard a commotion among his horses and quickly doused a smoldering fire.

"We'll keep some of Mahlon's cows," Alma Schlabach continued, "and some will go to other farms. I'd like to stop at the store in Berlin to get some extra food for all the helpers they'll have these next days."

After her appointment, Alma claimed to feel better and hustled through the market to buy flour and baking powder and sugar for all the rolls and cookies and pies she planned to share with the volunteer workers.

"We have plenty of applesauce canned from last fall," she added. "I can send some of that over, too."

When we got back at noon, Mahlon Mast and the local barn carpenter were looking at foundation blocks to see if they were okay. The builder took measurements so he could draw up construction plans. A few men with chain saws were cutting off burned framework at floor level.

I asked, "Do you need any errands run?"

Mahlon said, "My wife and sister would like to go to the Kidron store for extra groceries. And I'll ride along as far as the neighbor's to call on their phone for a bulldozer and a heavy tractor with a front-end scoop."

The next day, Saturday, the cleanup began in earnest. Fifty people were there to clean up or cook. A long-reaching backhoe from Shetler Excavating took out heavier pieces. Charred beams and still-warm grain were bulldozed onto a pile in a field. Five manure spreaders hauled debris and ashes out. Salvageable flooring and beams were removed. A lumber company man came to see how much siding and roofing should be set aside for this job.

On Sunday the site was clear and quiet. Mahlon's family went to church at a nearby farm. He was tired, but his father came over, and a sister arrived from Pennsylvania to cheer him up.

Here is a summary of what went on in two busy weeks to prepare for the new barn:

MONDAY—New beams cut at nearby sawmill. Foundation walls repaired where needed.

TUESDAY—Eight-by-eight-inch timbers arrived by truck. Head carpenter marked them. Eighteen men and women for lunch.

WEDNESDAY—Mortises and tenons cut and chiseled on beam ends. Sill planks laid on foundation. Fifteen people for lunch.

THURSDAY—Replaced big support beam for barn's main floor. Smaller four-by-four-inch bracing arrived. Twenty helpers. Date set for the barn raising.

FRIDAY—Still marking and trimming framework pieces that would fit together. Local lumber company cut rafters. Eight people in the morning, twenty in afternoon.

SATURDAY—Placed new floor joists where needed, and laid flooring planks. Thirty people.

In-between SUNDAY—No church (the Amish hold services every two weeks). Relaxed; visitors dropped in.

MONDAY—Bad weather. Six men finished new floor.

TUESDAY—Better weather. Assembled wall frames flat on new floor. Eighteen for dinner, thirty in the afternoon. Amish appraisers came to figure loss.

On Monday I learned how to chisel rectangular mortise slots in the eight-by-eight-inch beams. Someone with a boring machine drilled holes through the wood, and all I had to do was to chip out to squared pencil lines with a mallet and chisel. On Tuesday, I ran some volunteer trips to the hardware in my station wagon and picked up latches and roller-track carriages for the barn doors.

I thought I'd earned lunch, so I got in line when they called for dinner. We washed at basins of warm water set on a bench in the yard, dried our arms and faces with common towels, and paused to bow our heads in silent prayer. Then we picked up trays to carry through the kitchen.

Women in their white caps dipped creamed potatoes with ham chunks out of a hot roaster. Then they added creamed green beans, cottage cheese, Alma Schlabach's applesauce, pie, pudding, or cake (our choice).

We sat on benches in the dining room because it was too cool outside. When Mahlon's sister, Ida, came around to refill coffee cups, she told me the appraisers estimated an $80,000 loss. Mahlon had to stand one-fourth of that.

The other $60,000 was assessed among church members according to their property values. Landowners might be asked for seventy-five cents per one thousand dollars of valuation. A family with a typical hundred-acre farm worth two hundred thousand dollars on the tax books would contribute $150 toward rebuilding Mahlon's barn. People in many surrounding congregations were assessed to raise the money.

> WEDNESDAY—Siding lumber and metal roofing panels arrived. More wall
> framing put together and secured with wooden pegs. The wall to be set up
> first was laid on top of the others. Twenty or more people.

> THURSDAY—Extra Coleman stoves brought for cooks. Cleared barnyard for
> elbow room and good footing. Opened fence to field for parking. Boxes of
> nails and pegs set out. Thirteen for dinner.

> FRIDAY—Spike poles and hoisting ropes laid out. Food tent and benches set
> up in yard. Ten men helped. Women got cooking pans and paper-plate
> supplies ready.

> SATURDAY—The *Uffschtelling* (barn raising)!

Four men from Fredericksburg had seen me at the barn site and asked if I would bring them to the raising. They had driven over by horse and buggy two or three times, but on barn-raising day they wanted to be among the first.

When we parked in the field across the road at seven o'clock, it was misty. My passengers were wearing nail aprons and leather tool belts holding their hammers, measuring tapes, tri-squares, thick pencils, and chalk lines. Two had saws, one carried a sledgehammer, and another a long pry bar.

They were just in time to grab the last pointed spike poles and help push the straw-shed wall frame up and up till it stood unsteadily on one edge of the barn floor. I stayed outside and joined two or three others pulling on one of the ropes that fastened to the top crossbeam. We held the heavy frame from falling back as two dozen spikemen released their poles. Ropes in the other direction kept the new wall from falling on us.

There were holes in the sill for tendons on the base of each stout upright. If the tendons didn't quite fall into place, men pried the eight-by-eights an inch or two with iron bars and pounded them with sledgehammers the last fraction of an inch until they fell with a satisfying thunk into the sill. Others quickly nailed long temporary braces to the new frame while the boss-carpenter held a level against it vertically to check for plumb. That end of the barn was in place only a few minutes after seven.

More men were stepping onto the barn floor after unhitching their buggies and tying their horses to flatbed wagons in the parking field. At noon someone would throw hay on the wagons for the horses.

Other men arrived by the vanload from places as far away as Sugarcreek and Danville, in other counties. At the boss-carpenter's signal, they lifted another section shoulder high so spikemen could get the points of their poles under the frame.

"*Nau nuff* (now up)!" the head man called, and the wall rose, steadied again by ropes until it was braced in place. I liked being away from the crowd, but where I could still help with the ropes.

The next wall also went up in a coordinated push.

"*Noch meh* (yet more)!" the main carpenter called if they needed to shove slightly farther. Agile men climbed to the top of each corner to sock wooden pins through the joints.

Below the floor in the lower barn, a clatter of hammers began where stalls were going in. Older men who didn't want to climb tended to work there. Others started to nail siding on the new walls, so I carried boards to them. It seemed like a lot of milling confusion all around, but every area had an experienced foreman, and the total effect was massive teamwork.

> 8:00 a.m.—All wall frames were in place. Purlins were being lifted by ropes to carpenters on top, who pegged these horizontal pieces in place to support rafters.

> 9:00 a.m.—Long rafters were handed up to nailers calling "*Schpadde* (rafters)!"

I counted thirty buggies and thirty vans or pickups in the field. Weather was gray and cold, but luckily it didn't snow.

> Noon—Siding was all done and metal roofing (especially noisy) mostly on.

Two food lines started in the tent, out of the cold air. Four hundred and two men passed through (Ida kept count), plus three dozen boys who carried lumber or started nails in boards before the siding was handed to men on the job.

The main course was chicken and mashed potatoes with hot gravy and dressing. Jell-O salad and date-nut pudding were filling, but we needed to save room for all kinds of pies. Mahlon stood to say a few heartfelt words of thanks for the big turnout.

> 3:00 p.m.—The barn was completely closed in and work was so well along that some people started to leave. Jobs like spouting and making new grain bins went on for another hour.

I helped a steady old-timer get spouting ready by fitting the right lengths together and putting hangers on so younger men could carry them ready-made up the ladders to fasten along the eaves.

My passengers had to get back for their evening chores, so we drove away around four o'clock.

"Well, nobody got hurt," one remarked. "Sometimes somebody falls or something falls on somebody."

"I got my toe pinched when we rolled one purlin over," another reported.

The third rubbed his cheekbone. "I came near getting a roofing nail in my eye."

"I only overate." The fourth man laughed.

In the spirit of the day, I didn't accept any fare for their ride.

Early the next week, neighbors started bringing whatever hay and straw they could spare to put in Mahlon's empty mows. He led his cows back on

Tuesday and sent six cans of milk out on the cheese-house truck on Wednesday morning—only eighteen days after the fire.

"We still can't figure out who would do such a thing." Mahlon shook his head. "Especially with horses tied in the barn."

"This barn raising would have been a lot happier if the fire had been an accident," Ida remarked. "This was just horrible. I sure hope whoever did it repents before he dies."

"I'm ready to forgive whoever did it if I meet him face-to-face and he's sorry," Mahlon declared. "It says in the third chapter of Acts, 'Repent, therefore, and be converted, that your sins may be blotted out.'"

Meantime, however, he's keeping the barn door next to the road shut and latched.

7

Spring Plowing

"Is that the horse you bought last fall?" I called to young Obed Troyer when I saw him on a riding plow pulled by three big Belgians. They were turning fresh furrows through old corn stubble that April day.

"Yep, that's Prince." Obed pointed to the bay in the middle. "He's working out real well."

We both were thinking back to a trip several months earlier when Obed had hired me to take him to buy a draft horse. It was soon after he was married and had started farming at his bride's home place. The four-year-old horse had been advertised for $1,000, and Obed wanted to go that very evening before somebody else got there.

We found the farm almost fifteen miles away, near the Alpine cheese factory. The seller and his family were milking cows by hand. He finished a black-and-white holstein, poured the frothy warm bucketful into a milk strainer on a ten-gallon can, and took us to a stall where the hefty workhorse stood.

Obed looked the big gelding over.

"Er schur guckt gsund (he sure looks healthy),'' Obed observed. "Can I drive him once?"

They hitched Prince and a teammate to an empty manure spreader and rumbled out around the pasture.

Obed was satisfied that the animal was sound and worked well in harness. He dickered a bit with the owner and wrote out a check for $950. The next morning he sent a stock truck driver to pick up Prince.

Obed let the plowing team rest as he chatted with me. "That was a good buy," he said. "I've been to sales lately where good draft horses brought from $1,300 to $1,500 each. They usually go up when spring work starts. I had plenty of feed and hay, so it paid me to keep another horse over winter."

"How much can you and three horses plow in a day?"

"Two acres is about the most." Obed rubbed his short beard. "If the ground's wet or if it's too dry and hard, it's more like one-and-a-half acres. I started on March first, and it took me the whole month, off and on, to do one twelve-acre field."

"That seems slow, doesn't it?"

"Well, tractor farmers don't usually finish any sooner because they can't get started as early as horse farmers. Horses don't pack down the ground like a tractor does," he declared. "And with early plowing, there is better soil action. I like the fresh-plowed ground to freeze and thaw some so it makes the soil nice and crumbly.

"Also, I want to encourage earthworms and tiny living organisms in our fields. An early start gives the sun more time to perk up soil life as the weather warms.

"Giddap, Bonnie, Prince, Belle!" He started off with his plow set at a shallow depth for easier pulling. The morning air was cool, and the horses didn't breathe extra hard or sweat.

I had come to take Obed's wife and her mother to a quilting over by Walnut Creek. The two women carried a covered dish toward my car, walking past a freshly raked garden.

"I planted a row of peas," the mother said, "and scratched in some lettuce seed. Those are things a little frost won't hurt. I like to start carrots and radishes early too, and some spinach."

Mary Troyer looked like she'd have a new baby soon.

"We're going to have a haystack dinner," she explained as she tried to make herself comfortable in the back seat. "Each person brings one thing, like Ritz crackers or taco chips, grated cheese, lettuce, onions, hot beans, or rice. Our sister will cook hamburger bits and tomato sauce. Then we go around the table and make layers on the plate of whatever we want—as high as we want. There's usually cheese sauce to put on top."

Three miles along our way was a small fabric store, hitching rail and all. There my passengers bought a roll of polyester quilt batting and spools of thread. The little store had a modest COUNTRY DRY GOODS sign out by the mailbox and featured bolts of solid-colored cloth in the blues, grays, greens, tans, and dark maroon that Amish women prefer. I also noticed a good supply of cloth diapers and piles of strawhats.

Mary looked at a shelf of patent medicines and picked out Oil of Herbs in a tinted bottle. It contained peppermint, spearmint, wintergreen, eucalyptus, fennel, lavender, and juniper in pure linseed oil.

"We like it," she told me. "A few drops on the tongue is good for sore throat, cough, and even upset stomach."

Next we stopped at a house near Fryburg for a third passenger—Mary Troyer's sister. She'd been helping her twelve-year-old girl set out cabbage plants. The daughter was placing hot caps over twenty-five tender plants and pulling a little soil over the edges of each white cap to keep them from blowing away.

While our new passenger ran into the house for her bonnet, I looked at a few seed packets lying at the edge of the garden: Ithaca lettuce, Snowball cauliflower, Green Comet broccoli, Top Crop beans, Green Arrow peas, Fordhook limas. There was also a little bag of yellow onion sets and a fat packet of sweet corn.

As we drove on, I asked the sister, "Aren't you afraid the frost will get your sweet corn, planting it so early?"

"We know corn this early might get nipped. But most of the time it squeaks through. And if the first rows do get frosted, all we have to do is plant it again. This way we might get some early roasting ears."

"I'm going to plant as soon as the moon turns up," she continued. "I already put in carrots and beets when the moon was turned down."

Mary's sister was referring to signs in *Raber's Almanac* which tell when the moon is ascending ☽ (after full moon) or descending ☾ (after new moon).

"Root crops, you know, will stay underground better if you plant them when the moon is *unna ganda* (going down, getting fuller)."

"I know mother always planted by signs of the almanac," Mary said. "But I just go ahead as soon as the weather is warm."

"Well," her mother replied, "I noticed you had a lot of green on your potatoes last year because they were growing up out of the soil."

"Turn in the next lane," Mary directed me toward a big white house and barn.

I stopped beside their windmill. Two buggies were already there, and one woman was leading her horse to the barn. We had come sixteen miles.

"Sometimes we come this far by buggy," Mary said. "I drive to my first sister's and leave my horse there. Then we take her horse on to here. That way it isn't too long a trip for either horse. It takes about an hour and a half."

We set four p.m. as the time for me to come back and pick them up.

On my way home, I saw several teams of three or four horses turning the fresh earth. One man had two teams in the field. After he made a round with one team, he let them rest while he went the next round with the other horses.

By that time I felt ready to stretch my legs, so I stopped near a tall fellow in a wide strawhat, striding behind a walking plow. Both hands were on the handles, so his long leather lines to the horses were looped behind his back. There were two white horses, with a smaller black one hitched beside them. He stopped when I caught up with him.

After greetings, I asked, "How old is the white pair?"

"About sixteen years old," he said. "They're full brother and sister. I bought them when they were one and two years old. The mare has had three colts for me, but now that she's this old, I won't let her have any more. Kate has been a good horse; she used to outpull the gelding."

"Isn't it hard work to handle a walking plow?"

"It is if you're not used to it." The tall fellow smiled. "It is if the ground is stony or dry. But in normal ground, it isn't much more work than riding a bicycle.

"Plowing is more relaxing for me than shop work," he went on. "Sawing and nailing is noisy, and I get tense. Out here it's quiet—just the birds and me and Smoky." He nodded toward a gray dog.

"Well, King, Kate, giddap!"

As I went through Mt. Hope, I stopped for Swiss cheese and the weekly *Budget* newspaper. Two Amish men were waiting for their wives, so I asked, "Have you already finished plowing?"

"My boy is at it," one replied. "He finished eighth grade last year, so we have him at home all the time now."

"My married son is taking over the farm," the other said. "I'll help harrow when he's done, and when he's ready to sow oats, I'll go ahead of the grain drill with a cultipacker."

"Are you hauling people?" the first man asked as I opened my station wagon door.

I told him about the quilting.

"Oh—took them to a hen party." He smiled.

In *The Budget* several columns mentioned that late-March plowing was under way in various Amish areas of several states.

Marion, Kentucky

Gardens are being made. Redbuds
are blooming. Plowing is being done.

Viroqua, Wisconsin

We had some nice weather last week.
Farmers are starting to do some
plowing.

Guys Mills, Pa.

Not as much plowing is done any-
more with walking plows. This used
to be a favorite in cool weather as it
was great to keep one warm walking
behind the plow, even turning down
snow at times.

Late that afternoon while I was driving back to pick up the quilting ladies, I saw a teenage girl on a riding plow. She wore a head scarf for that outdoor job rather than a bonnet.

Farther on, six horses were harnessed abreast on a half-plowed field. Six horses together is unusual, so I looked closely and saw they were pulling a two-bottom sulky plow. A boy, about fourteen years old, got off the seat to pull out cornstalks that were jammed between the plowshares. The boy's father came walking across to help. He jerked the heavy plow backward a few inches —just enough to loosen the tangle. Then he and his boy pulled the stalks out.

At the quilting I asked the sisters, "What pattern are you stitching?"

"Come on inside and see what we've been working on," they invited me. The big quilt frame had room for three women on each side and one at each end. The youngest looked about sixteen years old, and one gray-haired woman must have been over seventy. They had crisp white caps on their heads and thimbles on their fingers. They were about half done with the quilt.

"It's a good thing you're here," Mary Troyer smiled. "My finger is pretty sore. This as an ocean wave pattern. It's for our youngest sister, who isn't married yet. She's the only one who doesn't have a family bedcover yet."

As we drove away, I asked Mary's mother, "How many quilts do you think you've helped with through the years?"

"Oh, I couldn't count them. But when I was a girl, we never thought of using new material for a quilt. They were always pieced together from scraps."

"Quilts weren't worth $500 then either," her daughter added. "The top quilt at the Mennonite Relief Sale brought over $1,000."

My passengers began talking about the dandelion sauce their sister had made for lunch. The fresh dandelion greens—chopped up with hard-boiled egg bits—were good, they thought, but the hot sauce poured over them had too much vinegar.

"I use lemon juice," Mary Troyer recommended to the others. "Instead of bacon drippings, I start with vegetable oil. Heat the vegetable oil, and stir in oat flour. Add milk or cream and some lemon juice."

"I leave the roots on when I pick dandelions," her sister said. "They're good for your kidneys."

The road back took us past Pioneer Implement Company, a small factory that makes new riding plows for horse farmers. About two dozen of the all-metal plows were lined up outside the building. The business started several years ago when horse-drawn equipment became hard to find. The owner is

Amish, and all his shop machinery is powered by a big diesel engine. He isn't connected to public electric lines.

At the second sister's house, where the hot caps covered new cabbage plants, I asked for five dollars for her share of the trip and permission to raid her lettuce bed later on.

"You can have some early sweet corn too," she promised.

Five miles later, at Troyer's, Obed was still out in the field with quite a wide strip of fresh brown earth showing. His wife paid ten dollars for herself and her mother. Then she went over to a dinner bell and pulled on its rope to let her husband know supper would be ready soon. He waved his hat in the distance and started a final furrow.

"We'll have early supper and then milk the cows," his wife said. "Now that the days are getting longer, we can't wait till dark to eat. I'll quick fix a jar of hamburger soup we canned last fall. That ought to keep him going for the evening chores."

She put one hand on her large tummy. "In my condition, I sure don't want to milk nine cows all by myself!"

8

Ascension Day

THE young Amish mother had asked me to bring her and two small boys back from visiting her parents' farm. Fourteen miles was a bit far to travel by horse and buggy—especially so late in the day.

I agreed to pick them up at seven that evening. While I threaded my car along the hilly roads of Holmes County at an easy pace, I looked at wildflowers blooming in the woods.

Now and then I passed a black buggy or a two-seated surrey, and all the riders were dressed in their best white shirts or white aprons. When I came to the Byler lane, it was rutted with the tracks of many buggy wheels. By the barn stood a bench wagon—a horse-drawn boxed vehicle pulled from farm to farm. It carried the benches for church services. Yet it was only Thursday, a nice spring Thursday in May.

"My parents had communion here today," Mary Weaver explained as she carried a leftover pie to the car. "Come on, boys, *dummel dich* (hurry up)!" Mrs. Weaver urged in Deitsch since her little ones don't speak English yet.

"Why would you have communion on Thursday?" I looked puzzled as Mary glanced at me.

"This is Ascension Day," she said. "It's an Amish holiday, so sometimes we have church then, instead of on Sunday."

Before we got the car turned around, an open buggy (with no top) came in, driven by a stout woman with a black bonnet and shawl. At the hitching rail, she climbed out quickly and tied her horse. She stepped over to a rocking chair on the lawn, lifted it easily, propped it behind the buggy seat, and tied it on with a length of rope.

"Her mother is eighty-six years old," Mary told me, "and communion is longer than the usual church service, so they brought the mother's rocker along for her to sit in."

Some men were starting to carry long backless benches out of the house. The benches did look rather hard to sit on for hours.

As we drove out the lane, I wondered, "How many people were here today?"

"Oh, about a hundred. The house is bigger inside than it looks. We had over twenty visiting ministers here to ordain a new bishop. This district was getting too big, so it was divided, and we needed another bishop."

I knew that church leaders are chosen by lot from among men members. "How many were in the lot?"

"Just three. That's how many ministers live in this new district. Somebody has to be a minister before he can be in the lot for bishop."

Three hymnals had been placed on a table. One had a slip of paper in it with an appeal to God:

Herr, . . . zeige an, welchen du erwählt hast, . . . dass einer diesen Dienst zum Bischofs-Amt empfängt.

(Lord, . . . reveal the one whom you have chosen . . . to receive this duty for the ministry of bishop.)

Each minister went forward to pick a hymnal. Then a visiting bishop opened each man's book until he found one containing the solemn note.

The choice fell on a fifty-year-old farmer who lives on the next road north. I tried to imagine how he felt when the slip of paper was found in his hymnal. This meant that he was obligated for life to be a spiritual head of the congregation.

"It's always a shock," Mary Weaver commented. "But it is a privilege to be serving the Lord's will."

Along the narrow country road, we went past Holmes Buggy Shop and turned onto a winding blacktop highway. Cows were out on green pastures, and the tender shoots of a new oat crop were showing across some fields.

"*Duh net* (don't)!" Mrs. Weaver scolded the older boy, who was poking a finger into the pie. His toddler brother was falling asleep in mother's arms.

I asked Mary, "Would you feel free to tell more about the communion? What does the bread look like? Do the Amish serve grape juice or real wine?"

She spoke willingly. "The bread is always a round loaf. It's always wrapped in a white cloth. Two deacons slice the loaf and then cut each slice in half. The bishop takes one half-slice at a time and breaks off a little piece for each person."

"White bread or brown?"

"It's always white. It's usually baked by the family where church is being held. But . . . you know that older neighbor lady who had the rocking chair to sit in? This time she wanted to bake the bread, so that's who did it.

"We use real wine," Mary continued. "It's red. The deacon makes it every fall from grapes. It's in a half-gallon glass jug, but the jug has a black cloth around it so we don't see the wine. Whoever preaches the main sermon passes a tin cup of wine, and every member sips from it."

We drove past a one-room school. Children were using the playground for late evening baseball.

At the next crossroad, a horse and buggy trotting ahead had its red taillights on, operated by a battery under the seat. I tooted my horn lightly, and the buggy crowded the ditch to let us pass. A couple with five children were squeezed into it, some standing behind the seat.

Mary waved and asked her son if he saw Danny and Jonas, about his age.

"They'll soon be needing a surrey for their family," she judged.

However, my thoughts were still on the communion service.

"Do the Amish still practice foot washing?"

"Yes, that's in the afternoon. We have four galvanized buckets—two for the men and two for the women. They're filled half full with warm water," Mary said. "I filled them myself today."

"Two people at a time take off their shoes and stockings and go to a bucket. One splashes the other's feet with clear water and dries them with a towel. The other person washes the first one's feet. Then they stand up and give each other the holy kiss on one cheek.

"When one towel gets too wet, they use another one," Mary added. "It takes quite a few towels! During foot washing, the congregation sings German hymns."

A mile later we saw two girls riding ponies, their braided hair covered with black scarves, and their full skirts allowing them to straddle the pets.

I asked my passenger, "Since the service goes on into the afternoon, what do worshipers at church have for lunch?"

"We had bean soup. It's in big kettles, and each person takes a bowl and fills it with a dipper. Then we had the usual red beets and pickles, and bread with apple butter. Some cookies, too."

"Is there anything else about communion that we haven't talked over?"

"Well, that's when we tithe," Mary explained. "Just twice a year, at communion, is the only time we take up a collection. The deacon holds a black bag open at the door as we go out after the service. No one knows how much anyone puts in. That's the money we use to help any member who is old or sick and maybe doesn't have enough to live on."

Near the end of our trip, we turned again onto a quiet side road. Walking toward us down that empty stretch came a solitary figure, a tall woman in a black dress, a crisp white cap, a starched white cape, and a long white apron. I slowed to keep from raising road dust, and in the twilight we passed so near we could see the cookies in a plastic bowl that she was taking home. She looked at peace with the world.

"Oh, oh! Aden is sick!" Mary cried, as she tried to catch some of her son's vomit with her own dress. "I know he gets carsick, but usually he says something before it happens."

"Shall I stop?"

"No," the drenched mother replied. "We're close enough home to keep on going and clean up when we get there."

"Does Aden ever get sick in a buggy?"

"No. There's so much fresh air that riding in a buggy doesn't bother him."

Mary's husband was out in the yard, playing with the older children as we pulled up. He led unhappy Aden gently toward the house. Mrs. Weaver asked what she owed me for coming to get her.

Since it was a religious holy day for her, I didn't want to accept business money. Instead, she agreed to take my family for a buggy ride the next week. She also insisted that I take the rhubarb pie along home. Just then her oldest daughter appeared with a soapy cloth to wipe up splotches on the car floor.

Nightfall deepened over the hills of Holmes County as I started back to my world of electricity and television. Beside me on the seat, as a reminder of my drive, was the pie with a hole in the middle, a hole the size of one small Amish boy's finger.

9

Corn Planting

It was June 5, and Abe Beachy was late getting twenty acres of corn planted this year. His children weren't old enough to help with fieldwork, and a wet spell put him behind, too.

"Thanks for taking this harness," he said as he heaved a bundle of leather straps and fittings into the back of my station wagon. I was running an errand for him to a harness shop eight miles away.

"It's torn pretty bad. I need it to hitch our buggy horses to the cultipacker. I'll keep disking with the big horses till you get back."

Abe was renting a farm four miles out from other Amish families. He paid the owner three hundred dollars a month and tried to still have enough left from his milk check to save toward a place of his own.

"Could you bring us back a fifty-pound chunk of ice, too?" he asked. "It's right there in a shed at the harness shop. Take along the lap robe off the hack."

A hack is every Amish farmer's light wagon with a stock rack behind the seat.

Then he added, "If you want to help, you could drive my road horses with the cultipacker and roll what I've disked before the lumps dry too hard." Abe had two buggy horses because he drove a peppy pacer that his wife was afraid to handle, so they kept a safe, steady trotter for her.

"You can stay here overnight if you want to," Abe said, "because we'll likely work late."

He seated himself on a riding disk pulled by four Belgians hitched abreast. Abe picked up the lines and tilted his strawhat against a bright morning sun. "Giddap!" he called to the team, and they moved ahead to smooth out the plowed ground.

The harness shop below Maysville was filled with wide tables, heavy-duty sewing machines, and presses to cut and rivet leather. A man in a smudged apron looked at the torn britching straps and thought he could mend them right away.

"This probably wouldn't happen if Abe would keep his harness oiled," the shop owner noted. "Harness that doesn't get used very often tends to dry up and crack."

He started to cut new lengths and stitch them in place.

I asked, "Is most of your business with Amish customers?"

"Only about 30 percent," he said. "We get orders for show harness, and most of our saddles and sleigh bells go to the *englisch* people. You'd be surprised how many of them come from town to get work shoes and rubber boots."

While he made repairs, I backed up to the ice house and opened its insulated door. Ice blocks tend to stick together, so I picked up an ice pick and made a few jabs to separate a fifty-pound piece. The chunk easily slid out onto the ice-house platform and into the back of my station wagon. I covered it with

Abe's hack blanket and went in to settle up: five dollars for repairs and two fifty for ice.

On the way back to Abe's, I stopped in Fredericksburg to buy a toothbrush. I was eager for the chance to stay with this plain family.

When I delivered the ice, Mrs. Beachy came out with flour on her hands. She handed me ice tongs, and I toted the square chunk through their back door and hefted it right into the upper compartment of a white icebox.

"Thanks." Mattie Beachy smiled. "We'll need that ice to cool some of the old hens we butcher today. I'm glad Liddy's out of school for the summer so she can help."

Liddy was ten and rode a bus to public school. They lived too far from any of the Amish one-room schools.

Abe let his horses rest and helped me harness the driving pair and hitch them to the cultipacker. This roller implement had a seat on it, so it looked like an easy job. My two light horses started out smartly over the fresh soil, and I just let my torso twist with the bounce of the roller. I'm not used to handling a team, but I didn't have to steer an exact course over the broad field.

By noon I'd caught up with the slower disk, and we unhitched for dinner. We gave the warm horses water, oats, and hay. Mattie fed us home-canned beef, boiled potatoes, warm crusty bread from the oven, fresh garden lettuce in cream, home-canned peaches, and rhubarb pie.

A bench along the back of the table seated three children. They wore solid-colored clothing; the boys had cloth suspenders, and Liddy had a full-length apron. Mattie took care of two toddlers on the other side of the table. Abe sat at the head, and they pulled up a chair for me at the other end.

Mrs. Beachy and Liddy wore white prayer caps all the time, and two smaller daughters wore black ones at the table. It's hard for little girls to keep white caps clean. All bowed their heads silently, with hands in their laps, before eating.

After the last pie crumb was gone, Abe said, "*Pattie nunner* (hands down)," announcing another silent grace before anyone left the table.

After dinner I stayed at the house to push a lawn mower while Abe disked ahead. About three o'clock I hitched up the cultipacker to catch up with him. By suppertime the twenty acres were almost done.

Our simple supper was creamy noodles with hamburger bits, called *Yummasetti*. Even though the Beachys had cows and used milk on cereal, the children did not usually drink milk by the glass. Instead, water was on the table.

This rented home did have water piped to kitchen and bathroom. It even had electric lights, too. Since Abe did not own the property, he was allowed to use the landlord's utilities. This was partly for insurance reasons; the owner did not want kerosene lamps burning in the house or lanterns in the barn. If Abe were to buy this farm, he would disconnect the power lines.

When we finished what they call "early supper," it was time to start the evening chores. While Abe, his wife, and Liddy milked nine cows by hand, the younger boys let me help them feed and water the chickens and pigs. We also pushed hay for the horses down through a square hole in the threshing floor. Then we fed two calves fresh warm milk from a bucket with a big rubber nipple near the bottom.

The bed prepared for me in a spare room upstairs had one sheet on the mattress. It was the custom in this family to sleep under blankets without a top sheet. Each window had a single blue curtain that could be tied gracefully to one side. The bedroom floor, like all others in the house, had no rug.

In the morning Abe helped me hitch all four draft horses abreast to rake the field with a spring-tooth harrow. That gave me a thrill—driving a four-horse team!

Mrs. Beachy changed from her pale-blue housedress to the darker blue garb she usually wore to town. She had a doctor's appointment, so Abe got her buggy ready. Two small daughters, in crisp dresses and black bonnets, went along for the five-mile trip. Usually it took less than an hour each way, but on this warm day, the horse was pokey.

My big team did well with the harrow. It is easier to pull, but had no seat on it. By afternoon I was tired of trudging in the hot sun. I made it to supper-time, though, and actually had a good six acres ready to plant.

For supper, we ate the first strawberries from their garden in a popular cold "soup" which each person pours over a slice of buttered bread. It is simply crushed strawberries in sweetened milk. Sausage from their own butchering and young onions from the garden rounded out the meal.

On looking around the room, I saw no framed pictures on the walls—just several calendars with pictures. One quote from Scripture hung in the living room:

*Und stellt euch nicht
dieser Welt gleich.*
(And be not conformed
to this world. Rom. 12:2)

As the evening air cooled, Abe asked me to take the horses out again long enough to disk over one low area of lumpy black clods. As soon as he finished milking, he walked out to take the lines so I could go in and read to the children. When I turned in at about nine thirty, I could hear Abe downstairs, intoning an evening prayer with his family.

Up at five thirty on June 7. My morning chore, while the others milked, was to curry and harness five horses. Then Mattie fried a couple eggs for me ahead of the others so I could get out in the field before the sun bore down so hard. While I made progress harrowing, Abe used his wife's calm driving horse with the spring wagon to bring seed corn and fertilizer out to the field. Two children rode along on the seat beside him just for the fun of it.

For dinner we had one of the old hens, stewed in a pan of gravy. Replacements for the old hens would come from a batch of two hundred chicks ordered last winter for their kerosene-heated brooder house.

Right after dinner, Abe took his best team for the corn planter, and I continued to harrow at a slower pace with two draft horses and two light ones. The field was not so wide, but it was quite long from the barnyard clear out to the road.

"That's the way I like it," Abe said. "I can make more headway, not turning all the time." As he filled the planter hoppers with bright-yellow seed corn, I noticed different names on the commercial bags.

"I never want to plant all the same kind," he explained. "We never know whether the weather will be wet or dry, or the season long or short." Then he reached for a coffee can full of red kernels and sprinkled a few on top of the hybrid seed in each hopper. "That's to make it more fun when we're husking. Giddap, Charlie, Bert—giddap!" The planter went forward with rhythmic clicks.

Harrowing was finished by suppertime, when I took my tired pullers in. Abe had almost three acres actually planted, so we all felt pretty good, and much lighthearted banter went on at the table.

"When we were kids," Abe remembered, "we used to take as many kernels as we had warts and rub a kernel on each wart. We'd tie the corn in a little bag and leave it somewhere without looking back. Then whoever picked up the bag would get our warts!"

We all laughed.

Abe did not help milk but went right back to planting corn until dark. His wife and Liddy milked while the boys and I did the feeding. When we'd turned the cows and horses out to pasture, Liddy spread a blanket under the lawn tree. With the smaller kids all sprawled around, we sang *When the Saints Go Marching In*. Then four-year-old Johnny volunteered this universal Deitsch rhyme, which he learned while bouncing on his father's knee.

> *Reide, reide Geili,*
> *halb Schtund de Meili.*
> *Geili schpringt da hivvel nuff,*
> *Boomp—fallscht du nunner!*
>
> (Ride, ride a horsey,
> Half an hour a mile.
> Horsey runs up the hill,
> Bump—you fall down!)

"Can I use your razor?" I asked Abe first thing on the morning of June 8. I was not joking. He keeps a safety razor in the bathroom mirror cabinet with a bristle brush and a tube of bay rum shaving cream. All men of his bearded church have clean-shaven upper lips—no mustache—and the cheek line is never shaggy.

Abe could plant the rest of the tilled ground himself, and I was getting ready to go home. I heated some shaving water on the kitchen stove. The stove burns kerosene, and Mrs. Beachy was frying the usual breakfast eggs on it.

I took a final look at the ice box, treadle sewing machine, wringer washer (run with a gasoline engine), and their remarkable little gas iron. That lightweight iron had a small tank of naptha gas behind the handle. Tiny blue flames kept the iron hot, without a cord to get tangled in.

Abe wrote me a twenty-dollar check for two days' wages. We had agreed that the third day would earn a couple nights lodging for me later on. That way I can use the Beachy farm as an escape when I want to get away from town.

Then I got back in my station wagon and cruised out the lane—back to my routine existence. For three days I'd shared in Amish life—three days I wouldn't trade for any number of movies or TV shows.

10

Buying a Horse

ONE Friday morning in June, Sam Byler phoned from the pallet shop where he and his son work. I could hear nailers pounding in the background.

"Can you take us to try out a horse?" Sam asked over the racket. "Dan's sixteen, and he's going to need his own buggy."

We agreed to meet right after work and head for Holmesville. An Amish dealer near there buys race horses from the track and resells them to local families who want speedy pacers. They either lag too often at the finish line, or they are past prime age for racing but still young.

The pallet shop whistle blew at four thirty, as I drove in. Two vans nearby soon filled with plain-garbed men toting empty lunch pails. Sam and his boy hurried to my car.

"This ad was in *The Budget,* and we want to try to get there first." Sam showed me his newspaper from Sugarcreek:

> Standardbred mare, 4 yrs. old,
> traffic safe and sound,
> a sharp boy's horse. $1400

"It's hard to find a horse that's fast and safe," Sam said. "Usually they're either fast and too skittish, or safe but too slow."

I asked him, "How old were you when you first drove a horse by yourself?"

"About ten," Sam responded. "I used to take the cart to my uncle's farm when I worked summers there."

As we traveled a quiet blacktop, we could see green leaves filling out the trees in the woods. Teams at two farms were pulling in the day's final wagonloads of new-mown hay. Some barefoot girls were picking peas in their big garden patch.

When the dealer's small barn came into view, its Dutch doors were open to the early summer air. Four or five bay road horses stood outside in the afternoon sun.

"*Hascht du dei vier yaehricher verkaaft* (have you sold your four-year-old)?" Sam asked when Jockey Joe Stutzman came out of his modest house.

"*Nay,* she's been waiting for you!" The pudgy dealer smiled. "She's the one there with two white stockings. She was doing a mile in two minutes."

Sam and Dan looked at the mare intently. The dealer snapped a tie rope on her halter and led her into a stall. Sam spoke calmly to the animal and stroked her head and neck. He ran his hand carefully over back and rump, talking all the while. Then he cautiously lifted each hoof by the fetlock to see if the horse would stand still for shoeing.

"It's time to take off those aluminum track shoes," Joe advised. "They don't hold their shape on hard surfaces. You could drive her over to the blacksmith shop and see if he's still working."

"Might as well see how she travels." Sam looked at his son for approval, and Dan nodded eagerly.

Jockey Joe brushed and curried the horse before he slid a buggy harness onto her back. He led the mare out toward a two-wheeled cart. Sam held up the shafts, and the horse obediently backed into place. Joe handed thirty dollars to Sam. "This'll pay for horseshoes if the blacksmith is open late. If you buy Dolly, you can split the cost with me."

"That's her name?" Sam asked as he and his boy sat on the cart.

"Yep, Dolly."

"Giddap, Dolly," Sam spoke quietly and held her to a walk. Once out on the blacktop, though, he clicked his tongue and gave the lines a mild slap. Dolly spurted ahead, and I decided to follow them in the car, but not too close.

It actually took me several minutes to catch up. The mare was stepping smartly, and my speedometer showed fifteen miles an hour. A logging truck came toward them, so Sam held back on the lines. Dolly shied some at the noisy monster but didn't hit the ditch.

A barking dog also made Dolly prance a bit. At stop signs, though, the peppy mare stood still without backing or balking. Sam handed the leather lines to his son for another fast sprint. Then Dan let the horse walk its final quarter mile to cool off.

At Honey Run Blacksmith Shop, a stout fellow wearing a leather apron looked up from the plow points he was sharpening.

"Would you miss supper if you shod this horse now?" Sam inquired.

"Maybe, but I'll eat better tomorrow if I get your money today," he replied.

"She has good feet," the stocky shoer said as he held a hoof between his knees. He pried the thin track shoe off and rasped the foot with a farrier's file. Then he cranked the handle of a blower to force air through his forge and heated four horseshoes to a cherry red. Grabbing one with tongs, he hooked the hot shoe over the point of his anvil and hammered out a toe clip.

Next he touched the hot shoe against a hoof to see how it fit. This made smoke curl away from the foot. He pounded the shoe some more on the anvil. The shoe hissed when he dropped it into a tank of water to cool.

In less than an hour, the smith had welded hard borium points on the shoes and then nailed all four horseshoes firmly onto Dolly's hooves. Sweat moistened his brow.

"En guta Gaul (a good horse)," the smith pronounced as he unhooked cross-tie ropes holding Dolly in place.

Sam and Dan were soon on the cart, and Dolly was pacing back toward the dealer at a good clip. The heavier shoes seemed to make Dolly lift her forelegs higher and reach out farther in a powerful gait. On one straight stretch of road, young Dan let the lines loose, and I clocked them at twenty miles per hour on my speedometer.

"Zimmlicha guta Gaul (fairly good horse)," Sam said to Jockey Joe at his stables. "How much are you asking?"

"She ought to be worth $1,400," Joe suggested.

"They weren't quite that high at the Mt. Hope sale," Sam haggled. "Can you take $1,200 for her?"

"I've got that much in her," Joe explained. "I could come down $50."

"Well, I could go up $50," Sam glanced at his boy.

Joe looked solemn. "Well, since it's for Dan here, maybe $1,300 would be all right."

"All right—for Dan," Sam agreed. "I'll have a check tomorrow when we come to get her."

No money or note was needed to seal the deal. Their word was their bond.

On our car trip back, I asked Dan, "What are you going to use your first horse for?"

"Probably go to some singings." He was referring to Sunday-night gatherings of young people at homes where church had been held that day. "And maybe to a wedding if I get invited.

"Some boys drive in Amish cart races at the county fair," Dan added. "That's where we see what our horses can really do."

"Maybe you'll be going to call on the girls now," I teased him.

"Probably no girls would want to see me," he said quietly.

"Don't be too sure," I kidded. "They're bound to like your horse!"

Sam paid eight dollars for a sixteen-mile round trip and thanked me for helping them go see Dolly.

"Tomorrow we'll tow a cart over there behind my buggy," Sam planned. "Then Dan can follow me home."

Dan laughed. "You mean *you* can follow *me* home."

11

Threshing Day

On the Fourth of July, while most stores and factories are closed, the Amish go about their farming and business as usual. Levi and Ella Shetler wanted to visit their married daughter, Iva, near Mt. Hope. All along the way, grain binders were in the fields, reaping wheat stalks into bundles. Some binders had as many as six horses abreast pulling them. Men and bigger boys, and sometimes girls in head scarfs, stood the bundles into neat shocks. They capped each shock with a sheaf spread out over the top to shed rain.

"Could we stop at Keim's chair shop on the way," Levi asked, "to see our son a few minutes?"

The shop was turning out bow-back oak furniture in high-production fashion. Some workers were sawing out seats and slats, and others glued and assembled the parts. I wondered where all the arched backs came from.

"There's a wood-bending place over by Mt. Hope," Levi reported. "They steam and press hundreds of bow backs for a lot of little furniture shops around."

When we drove on, I asked Levi, "Do you know what the Fourth of July is all about?"

"That's when this country started, isn't it? We're thankful to have a government that lets us live our own way. But we only celebrate religious holidays, like Good Friday."

At their daughter's, the first thing we saw was a big threshing machine stationed on the barn floor.

"They must be threshing winter barley," Levi figured. "It's always ready before wheat. Quite a few farmers grow barley because they can grind it into cow feed better than wheat."

The giant machine was run by a long belt from a loud tractor braced outside. Two men were tossing sheaves from a wagon into one end of the monster, and straw was flying from a blower at the other end into a far corner of the barn.

"We're going to the second house," Levi pointed ahead. "A lady there gives reflexology treatments. Then we'll go over to our daughter's."

So I parked by the second house and walked back for a closer look at threshing. When the flat wagon was empty, someone throttled the tractor engine down to idle and held his pitchfork handle toward me with a grin. To his surprise, I took it and waited for the next load.

"I'm getting lazy driving all the time," I commented as two dapple grays came in view. Their teamster ducked low as his full wagon came through the barn doors. When he stopped, I stretched my leg up for a toehold on the front corner and climbed the forward rack. Someone gunned the tractor, and the big thresher shook itself like a dusty elephant with a big trunk. The horses standing right by it were used to noise and never moved.

My companion tossed his strawhat off the edge of our load and began to fork sheaves down onto the feeder web. I was supposed to alternate with him, dropping my sheaf close behind his. I soon got the rhythm, and we kept a steady line of spaced bundles going headfirst into the metal monster. If I sent one sideways, the machine groaned and the tractor motor coughed. It wasn't bad if I made sure to fork the topmost sheaves. Pulling one out from under another was hard work.

In ten minutes we were standing quite a bit lower—right beside the feeder—and in another ten minutes we had to pitch *up* a little. We stuck our forks in the last two sheaves to push the loose straw and chaff onto the floor. Someone would shovel it into the machine after the horses backed out.

We must have done okay because the next wagon wasn't in sight yet. Levi's son-in-law offered us cold mint tea. I was glad to trade his fork for it.

About that time Levi showed up. "My wife wants to stay awhile, so maybe we could go on over to Tea John's."

That's the local herb fellow who gathers wild plants and concocts home remedies from them. His house in the woods is only a mile or two away.

"I still think threshing is best," Levi said on the way over. "We can cut wheat before it's too ripe. It cures in the shock without shattering out. When we thresh, the straw is broken up and makes better bedding. And it's blown right up there in the barn, ready to use. Combines leave all their straw on the ground, and it has to be baled and hauled in and stacked in the mow. A lot of good bedding chaff is lost."

At Tea John's, back a quiet lane, I looked over some of the bottles in his basement waiting room and read the handwritten labels:

Rescue Elixir
Extract of Nettles and Golden Seal
with Bach flower remedies

Lung Balsam including
wild cherry bark, mullein, Indian
turnip, Oil of Wintergreen

Hawthorne Berry Extract
strengthens heart muscles

Grumpy Johnney's Kidnee Compound
7 barks, wild grape, marshmallow,
cayenne. 10 drops in water
4 times a day

The labels gave his address as

Tac-A-Wah Herb Co.
Millersburg, Ohio

"I'm getting some of that Rescue remedy for our daughter," Levi said when he saw an amber bottle in my hand. "Just a few drops in a little water works. It's good for colicky babies."

We never saw Tea John because he was consulting with another visitor in the next room. A son who was about fourteen years old took care of Levi's purchase.

A buggy was coming in the lane as we waited to go out. There's no sign at the end of Tea John's driveway. People hereabouts just know where his place is, off one of the country roads southeast of Mt. Hope.

"He has a garlic and echinacea extract that builds your immune system," Levi said. "Just smelling it about turns your nose upside down. But we put it in empty capsules to take, and we didn't have much sickness last winter."

We picked up Mrs. Shetler and left before dinner because we knew there'd be too many threshers eating there that day. They were so busy that the son-in-law hadn't even had time to run over to Tea John's for the Rescue remedy himself.

"We'd like to make one more stop," Levi said on our trip back. "At my brother's bulk-food store. They just put up a new building beside the house."

This time there was a small sign at the end of his brother's lane: COUNTY LINE BULK FOODS. We parked away from the hitching rail in case a buggy came in.

The shelves were stacked with flour, sugar, and cereal in plastic bags, usually five pounds each. Macaroni and other pasta came the same way. Colored gelatin was in smaller packs. Raisins and nuts and candies were also offered in plastic bags, with white twist-ems closing the tops.

I noticed home remedies arranged on a separate shelf: Union Salve for burns, White Liniment for sinus congestion or muscle cramps, and PO HO Oil for toothache or earache. These are popular medicine-cabinet items in most Amish homes. There were also a few baby food jars with handwritten labels—Blood Poison Salve. They were filled with a lardlike formula from someone's family recipe.

Ella Shetler spent $18.34 for Swiss cheese and cornmeal and Grate Nuts—homemade crunchy cereal nuggets. Her sister-in-law who was tending the store punched in the prices on a small cash register that made the little electronic beeps just like the cash registers in town. My eyes followed two thin wires down from the register to a battery under the counter. Even the scale to weigh cheese and all those bulk bags was battery operated. It's not electricity that the Amish avoid, but being connected to "the world" by public power lines.

On the final leg of this trip, we passed a wagon piled high with barley sheaves.

"There were more outside strawstacks when I was a boy," Levi said. "The barns didn't all have straw sheds then. It took a good man on the blower and another tramping the stack to build it so it would shed water. We tried to make it lean a little toward the barn."

Levi is retired and does some harness repair in a home shop. One of his married sons has taken over the farm, and we saw him out with the binder, cutting wheat. Three of his older children were following along, gathering the sheaves into shocks.

During the whole drive on that Fourth of July, we didn't hear one firecracker or see one cap pistol. The Amish lived too far from any town to watch public fireworks that night. Instead, they would have their own display of bright stars and flickering fireflies.

12

A New Buggy

"CAN you take me and my wife over to Winesburg tonight?" Atlee Miller called from a pay phone. "Now that our family's bigger, we're thinking about a new buggy, and I can probably get the best deal at my uncle Ben's shop."

The sun was already low that August evening when I drove in Atlee's long lane. He and his wife, Anna, had already milked eight cows by hand after supper. They came out to the car with three boys and a baby girl.

"I've had my old buggy for twelve years, since before we were married," Atlee explained as we turned onto a blacktop road. "The wheels have been re-set three or four times, once because a car came toward me and the driver was paying more attention to a girl with him than to my buggy. He hit both of my wheels on the left side and bent one axle. It cost $300 to fix. The boy paid $100 and said to send him a bill, but I never heard from him again."

We passed a wagon with high sides that was hauling a cow. Up ahead we saw an open buggy (with no top) that had an extra horse tied behind.

"*Sehnscht da Gaul* (see the horse)?" Anna Miller asked her smallest boy. "*Vielleicht war's ahm Schmittshop* (maybe it was at the blacksmith shop)."

Farther on, we went past logs piled up at a sawmill. At the next house, a young woman was taking diapers off her clothesline in the twilight.

"Do you use cloth diapers or disposable?" I asked Mrs. Miller.

"Usually cloth at home, and Pampers when we're away," she answered.

"A children's seat is why we need a new buggy," Atlee said. "Uncle Ben makes a little seat behind the driver's seat."

We rounded a final curve and were glad to see the wide door of Ben Yoder's shop still open. It was a plain white building without any sign. People who need buggies know who in their neighborhood makes them. A couple of damaged rigs stood outside.

"One tipped over in a ditch," Ben told us when we went inside. "The other was a runaway when somebody didn't tie his horse. The horse turned too sharp and caught the buggy on a fence post."

Then Ben showed us a new surrey he had just completed. The two-seater had sliding door panels instead of flaps, and solid-rubber tires on the narrow wheel rims instead of steel bands.

"This is for New Order Amish." He rocked the black frame to show what good springs it had. The New Order differs from the Old Order by permitting Sunday schools, milking machines, and rubber tires. New Orders are the most progressive Amish except for the Beachy Amish, who own cars and meet in plain church buildings.

Then Atlee and Anna described what kind of buggy they wanted while their two older boys looked at all the tools, wheels, shafts, and equipment in the shop. Table saws and drill presses were run by belt power from a diesel motor. Hand tools, sanders, and paint sprayers were run by air hoses from a compressor.

"Headlights and taillights," I heard Atlee saying while Uncle Ben wrote down the order. "And a dome light!" he added.

The lights would operate from a battery under the seat. Knobs on the dashboard would turn them on and off, and there would even be a dimmer switch on the floorboard! Most buggy owners have an extra battery being charged at some shop or service station so they can swap batteries when their lights get dim.

"Plus hydraulic brakes, so I can help hold the buggy back going down hills." There are actual brake cylinders just inside the rear wheels of many buggies, with brake fluid running to them through tubes along the axle.

"Plexiglass storm front," Atlee continued. "Vinyl floor mat. Hand-hanger straps inside. Orange triangle on the back."

As a member of the Old Order Amish, he would get the standard iron-rimmed wheels and snap-down side curtains.

They chose a moderate-weight black oilcloth to cover the top, and looked at several colors of crushed-velvet fabric for the foam seats. Anna had to laugh at one color that was too bright a blue.

"*Ich gleich des* (I like this)." She rubbed a soft darker-blue sample with the palm of her hand.

Uncle Ben did some figuring with his pencil and came up with a price of $2,500 for the new vehicle. He would start on it after repairing the two wrecked rigs, so it should be done in six weeks. Primer paint and several coats of high-gloss black take a lot of drying time. While the one buggy is drying, he usually works on the next one.

A whole hour passed as they were talking over all the details, and Ben hadn't had supper yet. However, he seemed pleased with his nephew's order and gave him a four-foot yardstick (that long for good measure) with YODER BUGGY SHOP printed on it.

"Someone has offered me $1,000 for my old buggy," Atlee said as we started the drive back. "Hey—it's beginning to rain."

In the dark the boys were falling asleep, and their mother sang a lullaby for the girl on her lap.

> *Schlof, Bubbeli, schlof.*
> *Da Dawdy heet die Schof.*
> *Die Mammi geht un hold die Kee*
> *Und kummt net haim bis Maiye free.*
> *Schlof, Bubbeli, schlof.*

(Sleep, baby, sleep.
Grandpa watches the sheep.
Grandma goes and gets the cows
And won't be home till early morn.
Sleep, baby, sleep.)

The country roads were so quiet that we only saw one buggy and one other car the whole ten miles back. That particular buggy had a kerosene lantern for light. The lantern frame held a round red glass at the back for a taillight. That is what the most conservative branch of Amish use. Their buggies don't have storm fronts or even little windows in the side curtains.

"I like buggies and wagons," I said to Atlee. "But why do your people keep on using them instead of getting cars?"

He thought for a minute.

"We hold to the old ways. We like to do things like our ancestors did. We live close enough together so we can pretty much go where we wish with a horse."

"Is being separate from the world a part of it?" I wondered.

"Yes," Atlee answered. "We're told that we shouldn't hire a car to go places if it isn't necessary. But we are going in cars and vans more than we used to."

"A lot of English people admit that life is too fast these days," I volunteered.

"I like going by horse and buggy," Atlee agreed. "You actually see more from a buggy, and it's easier to stop and talk with someone. The horse-and-buggy pace helps to keep us together."

The Miller farm glistened clean and white in my headlights. Their wet collie ran up to meet us, swishing his tail. Anna carried her baby through raindrops to the house and lit a kerosene lamp.

Atlee paid ten dollars for the twenty-mile trip and thought it was worth the expense to go that far for a good deal on a family carriage.

"Come on, *Boova* (boys)." He picked one up and led the others out of the car. "You don't want the driver to take you home with him, or you might never get to see our new buggy!"

13

One-Room School

"I NEED to go visit some other Amish school," Peter Mast told me the last week in September. "This is my first year of teaching, you know, and I'd like to see how someone else keeps up with eight grades."

So Pete arranged for me to drive him several miles over to Hickory Grove. He had a student's mother come in to "keep" his school while we headed for the plain little building where Esther Yoder teaches. Pete had a dinner pail, and I brought a sack lunch.

"Esther knows we're coming," Pete assured me. "She's been teaching for years and has written a couple workbooks that we use."

We passed some boys walking the gravel roads, carrying lunch buckets, and wearing black hats. Farther on, a group of young girls wore bonnets, and some carried black umbrellas because it was raining a bit. Every three or four miles on this fall morning, we passed other small schoolhouses with lazy smoke coming from their chimneys.

Near the edge of a woods, we saw Hickory Grove and heard the first bell at eight o'clock as we drove in. The school, fairly new, is built of cement blocks, with a wooden shed behind for horses. Most of the children walk, but a few come almost three miles and use carts or a small covered spring wagon.

As we walked up to the front door, we noticed autumn leaf cutouts pasted on the windows. Pete and I hung our coats on hooks in the entryway. A sign on the inner door said,

ENTER FOR EDUCATION—
BRING YOUR OWN CONTAINERS

Esther was writing on the blackboard. Above the board were alphabet letters—both English and old-style Fraktur German. An eighth-grade girl showed us to chairs at the back. It was probably quieter than usual as twenty-five other scholars arrived and saw that they had company. Their names were displayed on a bulletin board of book covers—each pupil's name looking like a book title. Four books forming the first grade were titled "Ruth Miller," "Henry Miller," "Naomi Troyer," and "Anna Weaver." Most grades had three to five children, but there was only one seventh grader.

"Merlin, will you ring the last bell?" Esther asked a boy who had just come in the door.

Merlin pulled on the rope three times, then threw his chewing gum into a wastebasket and took his seat. It was eight thirty.

The boys all had similar haircuts, covering half the ear, and they all wore suspenders which formed cloth or leather Xs across their backs. Most of the girls had their braided hair up under black caps, but a few wore white ones. Their dresses and the boys' shirts were solid colors in shades of brown, blue, tan, and light green.

"Our visitors are from up near Apple Creek," the teacher announced. "Shall we sing our morning song?"

We're the crew of Hickory Grove,
    A very lively set.
We learn the lessons in our books
    And hope we don't forget.

Our schoolroom is a happy place;
    We're not allowed to fight.
Just smile and say good morning,
    To start the day off right.

Next they sang a German song.

Then it was story time—a Bible story in English about how David became king. Esther asked a few easy questions afterward, and a lot of hands shot up.

"We have perfect attendance today," the teacher said, looking pleased. "Some have been out with chicken pox."

"First grade, these are your new words." She pointed to the blackboard. "Say them after me: *store, going, please, today, lock, sock.*" Esther explained that *lock* is the same as *Schloss* in their language, and *sock* is the *Schtrump* they wear on a foot.

"As you read, write down each word as soon as you see it in the story."

Next she called second graders up to a bench to review vowel sounds. Third graders were finishing workbook pages and laying them out on a table for the teacher to examine. Other classes had reading or arithmetic assignments to work on, and spelling partners were allowed to whisper words to each other for practice.

Three eighth-graders were in the library corner putting state capitals on a large outline map. The lone seventh-grade boy was helping them, because geography was taught every other year for both grades. History was taught one year and geography the next.

"First grade, bring your books to the bench," Esther called. "Mary Stutzman, will you listen to them read?"

One of the eighth-grade girls responded. That let Esther meet with the fourth graders at another bench near the back. We visitors were close to this fourth-grade group, and I could hear them having trouble with the word *something*. They pronounced it more like *somesing.*

The morning moved along. All reading was in English. One reciter still had a few chicken pox marks on her arms. Teacher heard the fourth, fifth, and sixth graders read, and then she announced correct answers so they could check completed pages in their workbooks.

Ten o'clock—*recess*!

Some youngsters ran to the outhouses. Others played Ping-Pong in the basement, because it was still raining outside. In the basement was a big coal-and-wood furnace, and some of the children put foil-wrapped sandwiches from their buckets on top of the furnace to be warmed for lunch. Anyone who wanted a drink of water went to the outside pump.

I asked some boys, "Do you have any chores to do before school?"

Aden spoke up first. "Feed chickens and wash the milk pails."

"Water hogs and feed the horses," Joseph replied.

Mose smiled. "Make hay down and fill the silage cart."

"Bring in firewood," Menno added.

"Clang-clang!" Just one pull on the bell brought everyone back to the rows of desks—small desks on the left near the windows, medium desks in the middle, and big ones on the right.

It was arithmetic time.

"First grade to the board." Esther stepped to one side. "Who can add the quickest? Eight plus two." The chalk clacked. Ruth had a sum of ten first.

"Five plus four?" Anna finished first.

"Three minus two?" Naomi was first.

The teacher then handed a pack of flash cards to Henry and sent the first grade to the back bench to practice.

"Second grade, bring your rulers up to my desk," Esther beckoned.

Three scholars came forward.

"Now, how many inches in a foot?"

They checked their rulers to be sure it was twelve.

"So, how many inches in half a foot?"

They saw it would be six.

Teacher then laid a yardstick on the desk and had them put their rulers on the stick. They saw three feet in a yard, and thirty-six inches, too.

"Good." Esther sent them to their seats. "Tomorrow we'll measure some windows and tables, and we'll see how tall you are, too."

Third grade had a short spelling-bee-style contest on multiplication facts and listened to their teacher explain simple division.

Fourth graders did long division, dividing by two numbers.

The fifth grade had word problems, such as finding the average weight of turkeys that varied from ten and a fourth pounds to twelve and a half pounds.

The sixth had to figure out how much farther an airplane could go in twelve hours at 150 miles an hour than a train traveling at sixty miles an hour.

The seventh-grade boy had percentage problems.

Eighth grade had to figure out Charles Lindbergh's average speed across the Atlantic if he flew 3,647 miles in 33.5 hours. In fact, one whole page of their *Strayer-Upton Practical Arithmetic* was devoted to problems about Lindbergh and the *Spirit of St. Louis.* I turned to the title page and, sure enough, the copyright date was 1928, one year after his famous flight!

At eleven thirty the school eased into lunchtime. Scholars cleared their desks while one girl carried a wastebasket through the aisles for their trash. At Esther's signal, they all sang,

> God is great, and God is good,
> And we thank him for our food.
> By his hands we all are fed.
> Give us, Lord, our daily bread.

Teacher dismissed them one row at a time to get their lunch buckets. Youngsters returned to their seats or sat together on benches. Those who had brought foil-wrapped sandwiches went down to the furnace for them. Esther retrieved her good-smelling hot ham-and-cheese sandwich, then came to the back for a chat with us.

"How do you handle a boy who acts up?" Pete wanted to know. "I have one who won't sit still."

"Have him follow you around the room all day," Esther suggested. "Keep him right beside you till he's ready to sit down."

She laughed at her own idea, so we knew she had accomplished something like that with good humor.

"I don't often get cross," Esther went on. "If they get approval, they usually try hard. The less I say and the more I do, the quicker I get results."

She took us around the room to look at texts and workbooks. Readers were from Pathway Publishers, of Aylmer, Ontario. Their illustrations were of horses and buggies, chickens and cows, wood cookstoves, and other things familiar to Amish youths. There were also reprinted *McGuffey Readers* on the library table.

Arithmetic workbooks came from a print shop in Gordonville, Pennsylvania. They were designed to have children work independently, taking a minimum of the teacher's time.

Plain and Fitting English, dated 1982, was also from the Gordonville Print Shop. *Phonics Is Fun* came from Modern Curriculum Press.

The rain had let up, so most of the youngsters went outside and played a running game of prisoner's base. Three boys fed their horses. I stretched my legs with a walk in the woods, while Pete talked some more with the teacher.

Clang-clang, clang-clang! At twelve thirty we all went back in, and Esther asked someone to choose a song.

"Matthew Twenty-Four," a girl said, and the whole room joined in:

> I believe the time is coming
> When our Lord shall come again . . .

Then Esther stood with a book. She faced the lower grades and read *The Adventures of Unc' Billy Possum,* by Thornton W. Burgess. The older scholars didn't mind hearing a familiar tale again.

Then she turned toward the upper grades and read from *Coaly Bay, Outlaw Horse,* by Ernest Thompson Seton. The whole room was almost in a trance—English grammar broke the spell.

First graders put periods or question marks at the ends of sentences. Second graders at the blackboard practiced compound words, like *dustpan* and *milkman.* Other grades learned nouns and verbs or subjects and predicates, with past and future tenses saved for seventh- and eighth-grade students.

Spelling was more fun, with much busy practice and a lively spelldown. Fourth graders had to spell *whisper, useless, won't,* and *perfect.* Eighth-grade students had to know *enthusiasm, curiosity, hippopotamus,* and *gratitude.*

The afternoon went fast. Children were supposed to speak English, even at recess, but I heard lots of lapses into their home-learned Pennsylvania Deitsch. The school offers High German every Friday afternoon, in both reading and spelling.

They don't have religious education class, but they do read Bible verses, say the Lord's Prayer in German, and put Christian mottoes on posters and on the blackboard. One motto said,

He who looks up to God
Cannot look down on people.

At three o'clock, the scholars were dismissed one row at a time to lessen the scramble for overshoes, coats, hats, and bonnets. Hardly anyone carried a book home. They had plenty of study time in school, and plenty of chores and work at home.

"I was almost a nervous wreck my first year," Esther confided. "But I like children, and I like to read, so this is a good job for me."

I wondered, "Did you take any schooling beyond the eighth grade?"

"Just by mail," Esther explained. "And I go once a week to adult basic education, so maybe I'll get a high school diploma next year."

We offered our host a ride to the farm where she boards, but she wanted to stay late to duplicate coloring sheets. The small wagon full of scholars rumbled past, with an older boy driving. He let his horse trot as soon as they turned onto the road. Other walking youngsters waved at Pete and me as we drove away.

"Have you seen the *Blackboard Bulletin*?" Pete asked. "It's a little magazine for Amish teachers, put out by Pathway in Canada. It has some brainteasers, a good story for children, and lots of advice.

"It gave me the nerve to spank a boy who wouldn't stop pestering other scholars. He always found some way to push their papers or jiggle their desks. I was afraid to punish him till the *Blackboard Bulletin* said that sometimes a spanking is due—as long as there is love behind it."

"How much do teachers get paid?" I asked.

"I'd say from $600 to $1,000 a month," he answered. "It's not the greatest-paying job, and mostly young women do it until they get married. Parents have to pay around $500 tuition for their first child, but then less for each one after that. A family with four in school might pay $900.

"Once a year it's announced in church that all members who don't have children in school should pay a set amount for keeping it going. It usually comes to about $15 per person. Even unmarried members pay that."

"Well," I wondered, "what is so bad about public schools that makes the Amish districts go to all the trouble and expense of setting up their own?"

"Maybe they're not so bad for you," Pete replied quickly, "especially if you're going to be a doctor or an engineer or a high government man. But we only want a simple life, close to the land. We think we can stay closer to God with our own schools.

"We don't think we need all the science classes you have. We prefer Bible-based books. And we don't like gym classes where the children have to change clothes. We'd rather have plain old recess. And we don't agree with the way public schools have sex education.

"Then we suspect that some of the other kids in big consolidated schools are not a good influence on our children, especially in the seventh and eighth grades."

He looked at me to see how I was taking his lecture. "We just feel better having our own schools, even if we pay taxes to support your schools, too. We don't complain about that, because it's a privilege to be able to have our own."

When Peter Mast got out at his parents' farm, he smiled with satisfaction at a day well spent, paid me a modest few dollars for the trip expense, and invited me to stop in at his school anytime.

"Don't expect my classes to click along like Esther's," Pete warned. "I think we saw one of the best one-room schools around."

14

Husking Corn

IN October cornstalks had turned brown, and their full ears were dangling down from the weight of a good crop. I told Ammon Raber a couple of weeks ago, on a trip to his dentist, that I'd like to help husk corn for a day if he needs an extra hand.

Ammon didn't have any children—one of the few Amish farmers who weren't blessed with several youngsters to help plow and plant and harvest crops on the family acres. His land went back from a rural road near Benton and supported a fine herd of Hereford beef cattle. He and his wife, Sarah, didn't want dairy cows without growing boys and girls to help milk them.

One weekend Ammon found a phone while he was in town and let me know he'd be husking, if I still wanted to come out. Wednesday looked clear for me. When I drove in Ammon's lane at eight that morning, his team of Belgian horses was already in the field. I could see flashes of yellow as he and Sarah tossed new ears at the higher bang board along one side of their wagon.

I parked near a hog pen and walked past his white barn toward the cornfield. As I approached, I could hear the thump, thump, thump of ears hitting the bang board. Every few minutes Ammon would tell the horses to move a few steps forward, pulling the growing load along one edge of the field.

It was an overcast and chilly day. "What's the weather supposed to do?" Ammon asked when I caught up.

"*Drieb bis Middaag* (cloudy till noon)." I tried some elementary Deitsch.

He humored me with a few words in his dialect. I was able to chat a short while like that but soon lapsed into English.

We were wearing gloves to keep our skin from getting scratched up. "Which kind of husking pin do you use?" Ammon offered me a straight metal one that fits over the fingers of one hand or a wider wristband type with a small hook to rip the husks open.

"I'll try the small pin first." I slipped my right glove fingers through its leather loops. The pin's pointed tip was opposite my thumb and made it easy to pry open the husks near their silk end and strip them back. A quick jerk on the exposed ear snapped it off the stalk, and then I tossed it on the wagon.

"Do you try to get the silk off the end?" I referred to the dark brown tangle at the top.

"No—we're not that fussy," Ammon replied. "And if there are any mice in the crib, they can make a nest from the dry silk to keep warm and sleep more and not eat so much corn!" The way he smiled at his own remark, I wasn't sure whether he was serious or not.

We worked on three rows at a time—Sarah next to the wagon, me in the middle, and Ammon tossing the farthest. "Queen!" he'd call, and the horses would move forward, following the rows. "Whoa!" he'd shout, and they'd stop, chewing at brittle cornstalk leaves. After awhile the team seemed to know when to pull ahead a few feet and then stop without Ammon saying a thing. He never laid a hand on the lines. The stout-looking animals had full rumps, and the larger one must have weighed almost a ton.

"Queen is sixteen years old," Ammon claimed. "I bought her as a two-year-old when we started farming. She could already do anything, and she's been a real good worker."

By the end of our first trip up the slope to the end of the field, a mound of yellow *Kulva* (ears of corn) was rising in the middle of the wagon. The breeze was pretty strong at the upper end. Sarah opened a thermos of hot coffee and poured it into paper cups for us.

"This is a twelve-acre field," Ammon said. "I've already shocked the far side over by the woods. That corn we'll run through the husker so the fodder will be blown up in the mow for bedding."

A husker looks like a half-size threshing machine and runs by belt power from a tractor.

Ammon climbed on the wagon and drove the horses along a fence to the nearest side of the field. From this height, we could see another team in the neighbor's corn, with distant figures tossing a golden harvest onto their wagon.

We started working again, downslope so the growing load wasn't too hard to pull. I strapped the leather band of the wristhook on my right hand, to try it out. Now I could fling an ear in two motions: peel the husk with a cross stroke of the hook, then snap off the ear and let it fly all in one sweep. But I still couldn't quite keep up with Ammon and Sarah. Every now and then one of them would reach over to my row and whip off a few ears to help me along.

"Whoa!" Ammon had to shout at the horses. "When they're headed toward the barn, they don't always want to stop.

"This is an eighty-six-acre farm," Ammon went on. "It was seventy-six acres split off from Sarah's father's farm, and then we bought ten more later."

Sarah's father was a deacon in the local Amish district of some thirty-five families. He took care of money collected at the communion service to help needy members. The deacon reads Scripture at worship services and pours water through the bishop's hands at baptisms. He sees that older or ill members get help when needed. For communion recently, Deacon Coblentz had made wine from his own grapes.

"I got his recipe to make a gallon of wine for us," Ammon said, "just for medicine. If we have something like the flu, we take a little before bed."

We were nearing the pasture, full of grazing Herefords, and I heard a cowbell. "We have one Jersey for our own use," Ammon pointed to the brown cow. "Usually we have plenty of milk and cream and butter. But we've let her go dry now for a couple months to rest before she freshens in December. Without her to milk, this would be a good time to take a bus down through Tennessee. There are a couple Amish settlements there. Then we'd like to see the Smokies, and go on through North Carolina clear to the Outer Banks."

Again the horses seemed about to head for the barn.

"Whoa!" Ammon had to shout again. " 'Sis noch net Middaag (it's not yet dinnertime)."

Soon we were at the end of our complete round, so it was time to take the first load in to the crib. I climbed on the wagon and wiggled my shoes down through the *Kulva* till they hit solid bottom. With one hand on the bang board for balance, I flexed my knees for the bumpy ride to the farm buildings. Sarah preferred to walk. She headed straight to her back kitchen door and stayed inside to fix lunch.

Ammon stopped the wagon close to a slanting elevator—a long trough with slats on a moving chain that would carry corn up to the top of a crib. He started a gasoline motor to run the elevator and began shoveling the ears onto it with a steady rhythm.

Across the barnyard stood a nice pair of bay road horses, tied at a hitching rail. "The fellow who rents our basement rooms has a new blacksmith shop in that shed," Ammon said over the noise of his elevator. "He's just started shoeing horses this year."

I strolled over and took a look in the wide door. Another driving horse was already in there, and a young bearded man held its front left foot between his legs to trim the hoof.

The smith cut off almost half an inch all the way around with long-handled nippers. Then with a farrier's knife, he shaved off thinner slices from the flat bottom of the whole hoof. With the curled tip of his knife, he cleaned out each edge of the frog, a pliable *V*-shaped natural cushion near the heel.

I stayed to watch him pull a hot horseshoe out of his forge and shape it on the anvil. After plunging it in a tub of water, which bubbled and hissed, he hammered the shoe on with eight nails.

Ammon was ready to go back out for a second load of corn. His wife stayed in the kitchen. As we bounced along his back lane, the empty wagon rattled like an old-fashioned plank bridge.

"Have you noticed anything along here that we don't really need but still can't do without?" Ammon spoke loudly.

I looked at the white fence, the beef cattle, the winter wheat just coming up, the weeds in the center of the lane, an old tree with bright fall leaves. "No, I can't figure out what."

"The racket!" He chuckled.

We started another two rows, with the horses pulling the wagon right over standing stalks already stripped of their ears. We trod about half way up those two rows, pitching steadily, one nice firm ear from each stalk.

"*Huscht du ennicheh roteh Kulva gfunna* (have you found any red ears)?" I asked.

"*Yuscht ains* (just one)," he said. "I came across a red ear while I was husking to feed the pigs last week. I don't plant any red seed, so it might be cross-pollination from the neighbor's field."

A few of the ears today were nubbins or had moldy spots, but most were a good foot long. They started piling up rather fast. The thumb on my left hand was getting tired, and I had to favor it.

Ammon checked his pocket watch. "Oh—time to go in. It's almost noon."

We jumped on the wagon, and he swung the team around. He let Queen and Tom trot back with the partial load. My wristwatch said it was closer to one o'clock.

"We go by slow time," Ammon spoke over the rumble of corn bouncing in the wagon bed. "We call it *recht Zeit* (right time). I don't like to get up in the dark. The only thing I like about fast time is that the mail comes while we're eating, so I can sit around after dinner [the noon meal] and look at it. When you folks change to slow time next month, the mail won't come till an hour later."

Unhitched at the elevator, both horses went for the water trough and then to their stalls in the barn. Ammon forked hay into their mangers and poured a scoop of oats in their feed boxes. He also fed two other draft horses and the buggy mare he drives. Then we headed for the house.

"You can wash up here." He pointed to an entryway sink with hot and cold spigots. An icebox was also in the entry, away from the warm kitchen.

The kitchen was **big**, with a gas cookstove because they have free gas from a well on their property. The hardwood floor, varnished bright, led toward a dinner table by the far windows; kitchen and dining room were really one wide area. An even larger living room off to the right had a similar polished floor. It was easy to see how they could have church in the house and seat everyone on long benches, all within sight and hearing of a minister standing in the doorway between the two rooms.

"You can sit there." Ammon motioned to a children's bench between the table and window. "It'll make you feel young again."

No doubt that bench was used when relatives came with their families. Sarah sat nearest the kitchen, and Ammon took his place at the head of the table. Ground meat patties and mashed potatoes were in front of us. We bowed our heads for a silent prayer.

"Just help yourself." Ammon passed the meat dish and scooped a dollop of potatoes onto his plate. "If you go hungry here, it's your own fault."

The patties had been cooked and canned last winter in glass jars. It was tender ground beef from right on the farm. The potatoes were dug from their own patch this fall. I reached for hot shredded carrots and a slice of brown bread. Sarah had pulled the carrots just yesterday from a garden row covered with leaves. "Do you know what this is?" She pointed to a small bowl of dark-red spread.

"*Lattvarick?*" I guessed.

"Yes, apple butter," she said. "My parents just made it last week, outside in the copper kettle. They stirred about all day."

There was a tall glass of water at each place, but no napkins. The Amish consider napkins too fancy for their ways. I added some creamy coleslaw to my plate and looked around the room as we ate.

Each window had a single green curtain, pulled to one side. A china hutch was against one wall, and a treadle sewing machine stood at the south window. An upholstered couch was snugged against the inner wall, and a hickory rocker waited in open space near their gas-fired heater. A big clothes-drying rack was next to the heater to be used on rainy days.

"Since we don't have any boys to cut wood," Ammon said, "the gas heat is a big help."

As usual, no electricity came to the house, and a tall mantle lamp stood near the couch, supported by its base canister of white gasoline. Picture calendars were on every wall, and a seven-day chime clock rested on a high shelf along with two pretty plates and a kerosene lamp.

For dessert, Sarah brought on a big serving bowl full of chilled orange pudding.

"It's tapioca with orange Jell-O," she explained. "There are some pineapple bits in it."

Wow, was it tasty!

We ended the ample meal with another silent prayer and sat around talking a little longer. After all, the horses deserved plenty of time to munch their hay and rest for the afternoon pull.

When the clock chimed one, *recht Zeit,* we got up and headed back outside. Ammon shoveled our part load off onto the elevator while I walked out the lane to get the mail. There was one letter from a cousin in Buchanan County, Iowa, and the weekly Sugarcreek *Budget.*

A lot of *Budget* scribes included fall harvest reports in their columns:

Stanwood, Michigan
Nice fall weather. Lots of corn
is being husked.

Andover, Ohio
People are busy husking corn,
which is a good crop. Weather is
fall-like and a nice time to husk.

Port Washington, Ohio
We had the first killing frost.
Schools are having a week husking
vacation.

Baltic, Ohio
Corn husking by hand is in full
swing and beautiful weather for
husking. Meadow Valley School has
off to help husk corn this week.

Clark, Missouri
A husking bee and a wood-cutting
bee were held at the new ordained
deacon, Joseph E. Millers' yesterday,
with a very good turnout. 17 acres
of corn was husked by dinnertime.

When I returned, Ammon was bringing out the big horses and hitching them to the wagon. Sarah had cleared the table and was ready to join us. We could husk three rows again.

Those long rows had even bigger ears, but the sun broke through and felt warm on my gloved hand. We soon shed our coats, hanging them over the back of the wagon.

"Do you think Clinton will get in again?" Ammon asked.

"It'll likely be close, and he'll have an uphill battle," I replied.

Ammon doesn't like Clinton's stand on abortion rights. "He doesn't seem like a moral leader to me. But we don't vote in presidential elections. We just take what comes. Of course, there are some we respect more than others, but we pray for them all."

We made another long trip up the field, thumping corn and talking.

"The beef cows in pasture are on grass only," Ammon told me. "But did you notice six steers in the loafing shed? They're getting grain for the past month. I'll probably sell some of them next week."

Then, working our way back, we could hear a crushing commotion from far across the road, beyond the lane and mailbox. It was a huge combine, mashing through a tractor farmer's field, picking and shelling four rows of corn at once. They could easily finish twelve acres in one day, while Ammon was figuring on at least a week to do his field.

That self-propelled combine cost in the neighborhood of $100,000, while Ammon's harnessed team and wagon might be an investment of $5,000. Ammon's corn would finish drying in the crib, with natural airspace between ears. The modern farmer might have to run his shelled kernels through an expensive gas-heated dryer to preserve the crop for use or for sale.

I was glad to see the end of our field getting closer, and so were the horses. Ammon had to shout whoa every time they moved toward the barn or they'd keep on going.

Finally we were at the back lane. To my delight, the last three ears I opened were red! The wagon was so full that corn started sliding over the edge as Ammon Raber climbed aboard and took the lines in his hands.

"Go ahead," I volunteered. "I'll come behind and pick up any that fall off." I tossed a dozen ears back on as we made our way to the crib.

Sarah walked ahead and had two five-gallon buckets ready to fill with new corn for several fat hogs. The sky was clear blue now, and the trees in their yard were bright with fall colors.

"We won't be husking here again for a couple days," Ammon said. "Tomorrow we're invited to a wedding down at Saltillo. And Friday the neighbors around here are going to husk for a widow. Her husband died this summer, and she and the children are trying to keep their farm going. The oldest boy is doing all right, but they need some help."

He asked what he owed me for coming, and I said I was just helping, too, and glad to get a good meal and be outside for a day.

"Well, many thanks till you're better paid." Ammon smiled. *"Gross Dank!* And take those red ears along home with you."

15

Chris from Canada

IN November Chris Hostetler phoned me from Cleveland to see if I could meet him and his wife at the bus depot in Wooster. They both have relatives in Holmes County, where they grew up and farmed until 1974. With a growing family, they moved to Ontario for more land than they had in crowded Holmes County.

I can count on a busy day when Chris comes from Canada because he always has relatives to see and business deals to make. His sons are grown and doing the farming near Kitchener. He has a repair shop and does some horseshoeing. His daughter runs a small fabric-and-notions store for their neighborhood.

"It took about fifteen hours to get here," Chris said about their bus trip. "We crossed at Detroit."

He had three battered suitcases and a stout box tied with cord.

"Let's take this to Verna Petersheim's store on Kidron Road." Chris put the box in the back of my station wagon. We went out U.S. Route 250 toward Mount Eaton and cut south. One new home along the highway caught his eye —a lofty glass-front structure that we could look right into and see the furniture and cathedral ceiling.

"There's one guy with more money than sense," Chris let his thought slip out. Usually the Amish are slow to criticize.

We let his wife, Sadie, off at the home of friends near the county line and pushed on to the rural store.

It was at a conservative farm with a muddy lane and no flowers in the yard or windows. The only sign out front said POTATOES FOR SALE. Chris knew the way in through a porch door. The store was one room inside. Verna was a lithe young woman, wearing a thick, dark dress and high-top black shoes. We could see her through the kitchen doorway, stirring a pot on her wood-burning range.

"This is colic medicine from Canada," Chris said as he opened the box. "Gripe Water. A teaspoon in milk, and the baby's asleep!"

Then he bought a batch of spring-clip wooden clothespins for his daughter's store. "We can't get these in Canada." He also bought a dozen 3/4-inch lantern wicks.

The store room had a variety of kerosene lamps for sale. On the shelves were cake pans, teakettles, and dishpans. Dark-blue and black bolts of cloth stood on end, including fleece-lined material for winter jackets. Hooks and eyes were only eighty-five cents a dozen. Union Salve and White Liniment were on the counter, too.

Verna did her figuring with a pad and pencil and made change from a drawer under the table.

Chris and I drove on to Winesburg for an ice-cream snack at the town's general store, an old fashioned grocery-clothing-hardware store. Swiss cheese cut from the block was only $2.25 a pound compared to $2.89 at city supermarkets. Chris bought a five-pound chunk.

Below Walnut Creek we followed a quiet road past Chris's great-grandparents' graveyard. They were among pioneer settlers in the early 1800s.

Chris has a Gingerich genealogy book tracing ancestors back to early Amish immigrants who came to America on small sailing ships, such as the *Charming Nancy* in 1737.

Next we stopped at the E-Z Spreader manufacturing shop east of Farmerstown. They sold forty horse-drawn manure spreaders last year, some in new settlements as far away as Wisconsin. They are orange and green, like the New Idea spreaders of fifty years ago. They cost $2,700 each. Chris bought a plow point. Canada has only right-hand plows, and he needed one for the left-hand plow he took along when he moved.

We drove five miles to *The Budget* office in Sugarcreek. Chris is a *Budget* scribe for his area, so he handed in next week's column in person. It was handwritten on lined paper supplied by the newspaper. He gets postage and a free subscription for his efforts.

One of the editors gave us a tour of the composing room and said they have over four hundred correspondents from Sarasota, Florida, to Dunster, British Columbia. The weekly paper is over a hundred years old, usually prints twenty-eight pages, and has a circulation of twenty-one thousand.

We went back out in the hilly countryside to visit the last of his uncles. The uncle is on a typical farm, milking eleven cows. Some of the cows' names are Frieda, Polly, Star, Penny, Gentle, Sally, and Judy. A Jersey that looks like a deer is called *Hasch* (deer). There were lots of horse stalls, too, and we could hear someone shoveling silage down the silo chute.

Then we drove to a metal-casting place south of Berlin to talk about molding new shares for plows that turn sod to the left. Chris knew he could sell them in Ontario.

By that time we'd missed lunch, so we ordered sandwiches at a dairy drive-in. Holding a milkshake in his hand, Chris talked about milk-production quotas in Canada. Farmers need permits to sell milk.

"You can't start shipping milk unless you buy someone else's permit," he explained. "The price of permits makes it hard for a young family to get started farming."

Then Chris was ready to go back where we had left Sadie. He paid me twenty-five dollars for the fifty-plus miles we'd driven around. They caught the bus again a couple days later, but other friends went along back, so they hired a larger van to meet the bus.

Not long after that trip, I met a van driver from Aylmer, Ontario, who brought a load of Amish down to a family gathering near Apple Creek.

"Oh, everyone up there knows Chris Hostetler," he said with a smile. "Chris is a wheeler-dealer. You see him at sales a lot. At some smaller auctions, he'll even get up and do some of the calling for bids. I didn't know he came from around Holmes County. It's a small Amish world, isn't it?"

16
Butchering Day

THE stars and the crescent moon were still out when I stopped at Kaufman's Harness Shop early one December morning. Menno Kaufman wanted to spend the day helping butcher three hogs at his brother's farm down near Becks Mills. He was leaving harness and shoe repair in the hands of two teen-age sons who had finished eighth grade and were out of school.

"I always liked butchering day at home," Menno said as we headed south.

"Since I'm cooped up in the shop, it's nice to get out and help again once a year. They always start at sunup."

We talked about his work, and I asked, "What do you think of the new bio-plastic harness on some horses lately?"

"I still like leather best," he answered. "There's more of an art to cutting leather from hides and stitching good harness. The new plastic ones come all ready-cut. They're nice and shiny, though, so they're all the rage."

"Do you think I could stay to watch the butchering—and help some too, if there's anything a green hand can do?"

"Sure." Menno smiled. "You won't take any pictures?" That was his only reservation. The Amish think self-portraits show pride at best and are graven images at worst, breaking one of the Ten Commandments.

We could see lantern lights in almost every barn as we passed families doing their morning chores.

When we arrived at dawn, a nineteen-year-old nephew, David, was out on the frozen garden, striking a match to paper and wood under two large iron kettles. His parents and sisters had just finished milking twelve cows in the barn. They could see how willing I was, and right away Milo Kaufman pointed to a long-handled pump beside the house.

"You can carry water to fill these kettles." He gave buckets to David and me.

We toted pail after pail. Then I brought more wood for the fire, which was shooting flames up all around the kettles' edges. They used old scrap boards from a pile behind the chicken house.

Soon Jonas Kaufman walked across the fields from his small house. He's another son and has the wide beard of a married man. David is single and has just the merest thin line of a beard which he started when he joined church last year.

"Where's the twenty-two?" Jonas looked around.

His father waved toward a light rifle leaning against the hog fence. "I've been butchering for thirty years," Milo confided, "but I never could shoot one myself."

Jonas accepted the unpleasant duty. Seven nice porkers were in the hog lot, and he picked out a spotted one that weighed better than two hundred pounds. He knelt on one knee and aimed carefully at the head. *Crack!* Instantly the animal fell on its side. Milo quickly stepped over with a wide knife and stuck the hog in the throat to let it bleed.

"I work at the sawmill," Jonas told me while we waited a few minutes. "We cut lumber for pallets.

"This is the most interesting day of the year," Jonas went on. "If more people would take time to butcher, they'd find out how much cheaper living is."

"Now let's make a four-horse hitch," Milo directed as he fastened a hook in the hog's mouth and began to pull. He gave me his other hand so I could pull *him.* His sons did the same on the other side of the hook handle, and together we four slid the dead weight over rough ground to a wooden scalding trough.

We partly filled the trough with buckets of steaming water from the hottest kettle. In went the big pig, two ropes circled around its body to help us roll it back and forth in the trough. Milo added some stove ashes "to make the hair come off easier," he explained. He plucked at the bristles with his fingers to see if they were loose. When they were, we pulled the hog out onto an old door—and then the real work began!

With traditional round scrapers, we rubbed and stroked and pushed and scrubbed. A hog scraper is a metal disc shaped like a tea cup with a wooden handle sticking up from the back. Scrapers can be found in antique shops and museums. But in Amish country, they are still used a lot. My arms got tired, and I had to take off my coat in thirty-degree temperature!

When Milo thought the skin was bare enough, he hooked the carcass to a flattened tripod by the tendons of its hind legs. We all raised the tripod till the animal hung head down.

Then it was a matter of sharp knives and occasionally a hand axe or bone saw: tail off, head off, intestines out, liver and heart saved, lungs discarded, ribs hacked away from backbone. By nine thirty, two big and clean half-hog sides hung there cooling in the winter air.

"Are you ready for *Fischli?*" Milo called in Deitsch to one of the girls. *Fischli* were two red strips of the tenderest meat gently lifted from a back section. They were about the size of large fish fillets, and Rachel took them to the house to cook for dinner.

By then more help had come. Mrs. Kaufman's red-bearded brother rode in the lane on a two-wheeled cart after a brisk trot from his farm seven miles away. His name was Andy Yoder, and he brought along a meat grinder.

Jonas's wife walked over from their place. She had a small boy and a baby bundled up in a wheelbarrow. She hung her black shawl on a hook in the washhouse and traded her bonnet for a plain head scarf, ready to go to work. She started to make casings for sausage by emptying the hog's small intestines, turning them inside out, and cleaning them thoroughly in salt water.

At the same time, Milo's wife and one girl began cooking organ meats and head scraps for liverwurst. They cooked on a small kerosene stove in the washhouse. Two other daughters stayed in the kitchen to get dinner, cooking on an old-fashioned wood-burning range. Its black stovepipe bent into the chimney.

Some of us men scalded and scraped a second hog, while others cut up the first sides. They sawed off hams, laid out bacon, threw scraps in a tub for sausage and fat in another tub for lard. That lard tub filled up fast. My last job before dinner was to help Jonas scrub one of the iron kettles extra clean for rendering lard. We left it heating with a little fresh water in the bottom, laid more old boards on the fire, and went in the house to wash up.

Chief cook for the day seemed to be the oldest daughter, Rachel. Rachel teaches in a one-room Amish school, and one reason for butchering on Saturday was so she could be home to help. She dipped warm water from the wood-stove reservoir and poured it into a washpan for us.

Younger sister Lovina couldn't help giggling when David turned to wash. I followed her gaze, and sure enough—someone had managed to pin a pig's tail to the back of his pants! Everyone had a good laugh while Dave removed it and looked for a guilty face among us.

Ten people with big appetites sat down at a big table in the roomy kitchen. Most of us hadn't eaten since five o'clock. We paused for silent grace. Then we ate fried *Fischli* bits, bread dressing, mashed potatoes, buttered noodles, creamed lettuce salad, deviled eggs, celery sticks, and homemade bread.

For dessert we had Jell-O squares, tapioca pudding, mixed-fruit bowl, chocolate cake, and pumpkin pie. And all through the meal we had lots of hot coffee with cream and sugar.

"This is the best part of butchering day." Jonas helped serve his small son. "*Nau ess du* (now eat)!"

Everyone spoke in dialect to the child, who wouldn't learn much English until he went to the first grade.

"Maybe Adam's not hungry." His mother looked at the boy's runny nose. "He's had a cough. I put raw onions in his socks overnight. Sometimes that really helps."

It was so warm in the kitchen-dining room that Milo opened a window.

His set of brass weather dials on the wall registered 83 degrees inside, 30.66 units of barometric pressure, 41 percent humidity, and 32 degrees outside. A framed plaque nearby read,

> *Herr, weise mir deinen Weg*
> *und leite mich auf richtiger Bahn.*
> (Lord, show me your way
> and lead me on a right path. Ps. 27:11)

When the family conversation drifted into Deitsch, my ears caught English words that have crept into their dialect:

> *Rudy un Leroy vare um squabbleh heit. Sie waare um pony reide. Da Rudy hot gsaat,*
> *"Du bischt nau supposed ab kumme." No hot d' Leroy gsaat, "Ich bin noch net ready."*
> *Da Rudy var sorta baas. No hot d'Leroy gsaat, "Was iss dei hurry?" Da Rudy hot*
> *gsaat, "Mei hinne end iss kalt."*

> (Rudy and Leroy were squabbling today. They were pony riding. Rudy said,
> "Now you're supposed to come off." Then Leroy said, "I'm not yet ready."
> Rudy was sort of angry. Then Leroy said, "What's your hurry?" Rudy said,
> "My hind end is cold.")

Outside again, the big hot kettle was waiting, and Jonas dumped the tub of fat into the kettle to make lard. That little bit of boiling water in the bottom kept the white chunks from sticking to the iron.

I brought more firewood and took a few turns stirring with a metal rod. If we didn't stir, a pocket of steam might form down in the simmering mass and explode with force. Jonas told me that people have actually been killed from standing near an untended pot of lard.

"But don't spill it over the edge, either," he cautioned, "or the whole kettle could catch on fire."

I was happy to let him stir most of the time!

The chunks of fat shrank and browned as more lard cooked out. After awhile a bubbly foam covered the top. It was easier to stir, and all the dangerous water had boiled out.

"Just tease it a little." Jonas gave me the rod again. "We'll make some potato chips."

Rachel had brought out a small pan of sliced potatoes, and her brother threw the raw slices into the bubbly pot.

"That will make the lard clean," he said.

Meanwhile, women in the washhouse were trimming cooked meat off the liverwurst pieces that had cooled over noon. Into the wurst go leg meat and stomach lining, among other things. They put all those scraps back into the meat juices and added salt, to cook for ten minutes more.

Suddenly the lard was ready. Its bubbly layer of foam went down so we could see the potato chips floating on top. Chunks of fat had shriveled into brown cracklings. Jonas and I slid a long pole through the big kettle handle and carefully lifted the hot lard off its fire.

Milo placed a sausage press nearby. He had a clean white cloth tied over its spout for a strainer. As he dipped the hot liquid with a saucepan and poured it through the press, clear steaming oil drained through into a clean pail.

The browned cracklings went in the press, too, and when it got full, Menno cranked the lid down to squeeze out more lard.

Milo carried that lard pail to the washhouse several times and filled nine crocks there with pure lard for his family this coming year. And the potato chips—they were laid out on a plate for us all to sample right then.

While Milo filled crocks, Uncle Andy and David had Andy's meat grinder going for sausage. A whole tub of raw pork scraps had to be ground up. I took my turn on the grinder handle, and my arm got plenty tired!

Just when the sausage meat was all ground, the cooked liverwurst meat was ready to grind up, too!

Luckily, Lovina came out about then with cookies and coffee for a little break. She even brought the rest of the pies we hadn't been able to finish at dinner. And most everyone nibbled a few pieces of cracklings or fresh liverwurst, too. No wonder if someone has an upset stomach on butchering day!

The women put salt and pepper and spices over the pile of ground-up scraps and worked it in with their hands.

The ground liverwurst filled sixteen glass jars, which Mrs. Kaufman would preserve on Monday. She and Lovina would also can the spare ribs, chopped into small pieces, and the long tenderloin strips.

On Monday, too, the women would mix a curing powder to smear over the hams. The glaze would have salt, saltpeter, pepper, flour, and brown sugar in it. The hams were to cure for two weeks, then hang in a hickory-fired smokehouse for four days. That's where some of the sausage would hang, too.

That was the last part of butchering day—stuffing sausage. Milo brought in the press. Jonas got the casings his wife had cleaned. Andy Yoder slipped the casings onto the spout. Menno crammed ground meat into the press and screwed the top down. Out shot a stream of sausage into the transparent casing. The long links dropped into a big dishpan, which David kept turning so the sausage coiled around on itself like a thick rope.

They paused to put more meat in the press and more casing on the spout. Then they squeezed out more coils again, with Uncle Andy making remarks in Deitsch that had the other men laughing. The dishpan was heaping when they finished. Except for cleaning up, the job was done.

Andy packed his grinder on his road cart and got his horse from the barn. Jonas's wife put her children in the wheelbarrow for her short push home. Mrs. Kaufman gave me three feet of country sausage to take back to town. Menno had some too, and he would be back later for one smoked ham and one crock of cooled lard.

"Would you like to come again when we butcher a beef?" Milo wondered. So maybe I hadn't been too much in the way after all. As Menno and I toted sausage links to the car, I felt as if, for the last twelve hours, we'd stepped back through time to a century ago.

17

Farewell

THE daily newspaper's obituary column printed Amanda Burkholder's name on Thursday and said services would be at her home at nine on Saturday morning. She died at age eighty-six after an extended illness. Her husband, Yost, and six children mourned her passing. She also had forty-seven grandchildren and forty-eight great-grandchildren.

"She was a member of the Old Order Amish," the column stated. "Friends may call anytime at the residence."

I first knew the Burkholders years ago when they bought a second farm with an old house and barn on it. The house was empty, so Yost let my family live in it for several months while he worked to fix up the barn. One of their boys started farming next spring, but meanwhile we watched over the place. Most of the neighbors were Amish, and some girls from the next farm north occasionally helped my wife when our children were small.

The father of those hired girls still lives between me and the Burkholder home, so Thursday evening I asked if he wanted to ride along to the open calling hours for Amanda. The weather was cold and snowy; he was glad to change clothes and go with me rather than take his buggy the next day. He is Monroe Mast, father of the farmer whose barn burned. His wife had passed away five years earlier.

"There's nothing more certain than death," Monroe reflected as we rode toward Yost's. "We hope we can go on to heaven—there's nothing better than that. And there's nothing worse than hell. That makes judgment pretty scary, doesn't it?"

"Yes," I responded, "so we'd better pay attention to how Jesus said we should live."

"My wife had a lot of patience and a lot of love for us," he added. "I think we'll be together again. We're not perfect, but the Lord is merciful."

When we got to the Burkholder driveway, it was choked with vans. We parked at one side of the road. Buggies were jammed in around the barn. Someone pointed to a back porch door as the best way in.

The first room was filled with women seated on benches. A table was piled with black coats and hats. The line of visitors threaded through a second room of men. We shook hands as we went until we reached a little room where Amanda's small frame in black dress and white cap was laid on a narrow table or platform. She looked worn and gray in the glare of a gas-mantle floor lamp.

We moved on out to another room and found space on more benches. I was next to a son-in-law holding one of the great-grandchildren. Beside him was a twenty-seven-year-old grandson who told me how Amanda had been in bed most of the year. She'd been an Alzheimer's victim and became too weak to eat or even drink. Dr. Lehman had came from his Mount Eaton office to give an antibiotic shot for pneumonia. Yesterday she finally slipped into a coma.

The next day was no doubt full of similar visiting, especially by relatives and longtime friends who came from a distance.

Saturday morning I had a trip with two men and their wives who were going to help a newly married brother fix up his home. After delivering them, I drove to the funeral three or four miles away. It was so crowded at the main house that the overflow nearly filled a grandson's place back the next lane—with a second set of preachers there.

When I came in the second house, a minister from southern Ohio was standing in the doorway between two rooms. He had helped start a new settlement near Gallipolis. He spoke Deitsch—with some Scripture in High German—in a singsong rhythmical tone. Then he dropped his voice almost to a whisper for awhile before building back up with force. He talked about living in ways that please God so we, too, might be prepared to meet our Maker.

After half an hour, another minister took the floor. He has a local harness shop near one of the busy highways that run through this Amish territory. For the record, he told how Amanda was born in 1909 near Mt. Hope and married Yost Burkholder in 1939. He listed her children and number of descendants, and spoke of her as a devoted homemaker and a fine example of Christian faithfulness.

The minister then said that the story of Adam and Eve explains why death came to paradise: their disobedience. And the story of Noah and the ark shows that obedience can spare us much woe.

One thing I liked about this funeral service: it was attended by people from different Amish groups who don't normally worship together. More-conservative Amish men with longer hair were sitting beside main-body Old Order Amish neighbors, who allow battery lights on their buggies. Both groups were joined on this occasion by New Order Amish, who have milking machines and a band of solid rubber on their buggy wheels.

There are more serious disagreements—like whether to have Sunday schools or how strictly to enforce church rules. But at funerals and barn raisings, they put differences aside and support each other. They make their *englisch* friends welcome, too. The second minister ended by asking us to kneel while he read a long prayer from *Die ernsthafte Christenpflicht*, compiled three hundred years ago in Europe, before the Amish came to America:

> Oh loving Father, . . . you have now redeemed her from the
> misery of this sinful world, and brought her sorrows to an
> end, and as we hope, have given her a blessed end.

Then we all walked through a stiff, cold wind to the main house for a final viewing. Amanda was at rest in a shaped poplar coffin made just to fit her length. The outside was polished, and the inside was lined with white cloth. A long line was still filing into the house as some of us came out.

Then the coffin maker closed a lid over the body and tightened the cover with screws. Four pallbearers carried Mrs. Burkholder to a spring wagon for the procession to Yoder cemetery, a mile away. Most went in buggies because of the wind, but some walked.

At the burial site, the pallbearers put two stout poles under the coffin to support it over the open grave. Then they looped long straps around each end. When the pallbearers lifted the coffin by those straps, someone pulled out the support poles, and the coffin was slowly lowered until it rested below. Next a large rough covering box was placed over the smooth coffin. There were no flowers or artificial turf.

When all was ready, the local bishop read from 1 Thessalonians, chapter 4. All men and boys present removed their hats as he spoke. "If we believe Jesus died and rose again, even so those also who sleep in Jesus will God bring with him."

Small hymn books had been passed through the outdoor crowd, and the bishop spoke this traditional verse from it:

> *Gute Nacht, ihr meine Lieben,*
> *Gute Nacht, ihr Herzenfreund.*
>
> (Good night, my loved ones,
> Good night, you dearest friends.)

Then the whole group repeated that verse by singing it in a slow chant as the pallbearers took shovels and began to fill the grave. The bishop read a second verse, then everyone sang it:

> *Gute Nacht, die sich betrüben,*
> *Und aus Lieb für mich jetzt weint!*
>
> (Good night, you who are grieving,
> And out of love for me now weep!)

They kept reading and singing till the grave was a mound at their feet.

> Although I leave you now,
> And my flesh you lay below,
> It will be raised again,
> And I'll see you evermore.

The bishop spoke a few words of comfort and encouragement to family members. Finally he asked everyone to pray the Lord's Prayer together, which they did in quiet tones in German.

Then family and friends calmly returned to their buggies or started walking back into the steady wind. Because of the harsh weather, two Amish men I knew accepted a ride in my car.

"She was a strong woman most of her life," one said, "hardly ever sick. She liked her family, but she was strict with them."

"She was a quiet person," the other remarked. "She wouldn't want publicity about herself. She was more concerned about her standing with God than with what people thought of her."

They invited me back to the Burkholder farmhouse for hot coffee and a simple setting of cold cuts, red beets, and soft peanut-butter spread on bread. The bereaved family had a throng with them all afternoon, and the comfort of a close community as they adjusted to the vacant place in their hearts.

18

Another Year

ONE of Enos Miller's older boys scuffed through light snow on his way toward the barn. He carried a pitchfork to push hay out for heifers in the loafing lot, and his beagle pup tagged along in case the youth stirred up any mice.

The boy, in black hat and denim jacket, waved to me as I drove up on that last day of the year and parked by their windmill, waiting for his mother to come out. She needed a ride this cold morning to take her newest baby to a country therapist. She'd gone there by horse and buggy a few days earlier, but the man wasn't home. Now it was too chilly for the ten-mile trip with an infant, so she hired me to take them by car.

"Nathan just cries most of the night," Mrs. Miller explained as she settled in the front seat, holding her bundled child and loosening her shawl. "Something must be bothering him."

We headed out the lane and onto a blacktop road.

"I like winter for a change," Clara Miller said. "When I'm all done with the canning, I just put wood in the stove and sit at the sewing machine in a south window and watch birds at the feeder. Winter is relaxing for me."

We passed a nice dappled team pulling a wagon full of yellow ear corn toward Maysville mill. Almost every mile we saw horse-drawn manure spreaders scattering their loads over white fields now that the ground was frozen again. Buggy horses on the road snorted steam, and those tied at hitching rails had blankets over their backs.

Nathan fussed quite a bit and kept moving his arms and kicking.

"We turn in here." My passenger pointed to a short lane. The red barn and white house looked like others in the neighborhood. There was no sign out front. An older Amish farmer there offers his health help without fanfare, and fellow church folks all around know where he lives.

"He doesn't charge any certain amount," Clara said. "Whoever goes for a treatment just gives him whatever they think it's worth to them."

I pulled in beside a woodshed and two black buggies. As soon as Mrs. Miller took her baby into the house, I heard hammering over by the barn. A bearded young man was picking out lumber from a pile of broken pallets to build a small hog house.

"This is a truckload of scrap wood from Kidron Body," the fellow said. "They dumped it here free. If they take it to a landfill, they have to pay to dump it. I can get a lot of short two-by-fours out of it. Then what I can't use, we'll cut up for firewood."

I passed him a few boards to nail on the shed roof until Mrs. Miller came out.

She told me what the therapist had found. "Nathan had a hip out of place. That reminds me of years ago. Our oldest boy didn't walk when he was almost a year and a half old. We took him for a treatment, and he started walking that very night!"

On our way back, we stopped for groceries at the Kidron Town and Country Store. A hefty man was tying his horse at the hitching rail, and I asked how far he'd come.

"Oh, about nine miles," he figured. "This nippy weather is good for horses. They feel pretty peppy."

When a grocery boy brought Clara's cart out, some of her selections looked anything but old-fashioned: disposable diapers, Ruffles Potato Chips, split-top bread, and frozen meatloaf dinners! But she also had staples like head lettuce, noodles, sugar, and oranges.

"I came for sauerkraut," she explained. "We have sauerkraut and mashed potatoes for New Year's Eve supper, usually with wieners or pork chops. Then we play games and sing songs, especially the New Year's song at midnight:

> *Heut fänget an das neue Jahr,*
> *Mit neuem Gnadenschein;*
> *Wir loben Alle unsern Gott,*
> *Und singen insgemein.*
>
> (Today begins the New Year,
> With fresh new light of grace;
> We all do praise our God
> And sing in full accord.)

From the store, we drove a mile west and stopped at her sister's house to iron a Sunday dress that Mrs. Miller had brought along.

"I had a fire accident with my gas iron at home," she said. "I had to quick throw it out the window. So I need to use her iron to get this dress ready for a wedding on Thursday."

Clara's sister had several drip-dry dresses of her own hanging on the line outside, and little fringes of icicles were forming along the hems. The dresses were dark blue, aqua, or tan, with no buttons or snaps. Amish women close their dresses with straight pins. I often find a pin or two on the seat or floor of my station wagon when I get home from giving them rides.

"Come on in, too," Clara motioned toward her sister's porch. "It's too cold to wait out here."

As soon as she opened the door, a fresh-bread aroma welcomed us inside. Anna Wengerd was pulling four loaves out of the oven. Three small boys waited for her to slice some warm crusts and butter them as a winter treat. She offered me one, too, and I couldn't refuse. It was mouth watering!

Clara set up the ironing board and looked for a match. The little iron she lit was a lightweight Coleman gas model with instant blue flames. It was easy to handle, but a gas leak or spill can cause trouble.

The sisters chatted in Deitsch while Clara pressed her blue Sunday dress. I walked across a polished living-room floor to look at their bookshelf. There were books in German, such as Luther's *Bibel,* Ben Raber's *Almanac, Martyrs Mirror,* and the *Ausbund* (thick hymnal); and several in English, such as *Rosanna of the Amish, Back to Eden,* and *The Miller History.*

Ironing done, Mrs. Miller carried her sleeping boy to the car, and I brought the carefully folded dress.

"Anna's man works on a carpenter crew," Clara told me. "They want to start a cabinet shop someday so he'll be home with their boys more. It's best for the children to have both parents at home. But a lot more men are working at sawmills and even factories these days."

Just before the Miller farm we noticed a group of buggies in a neighbor's barnyard and several women plucking chicken feathers outside the kitchen.

"This is where the wedding will be," Clara explained. "It's the oldest Keim girl. She was our *Maud* when Nathan was born. She'll make Emanuel Schrock a *gute Froh* (good wife)."

"Yes," I agreed. "I took her to Lakeville a couple times where she was teaching."

"That's where the Schrock boy is from," Clara said. "Now we know why she didn't teach again this fall."

At the Miller farm her only daughter came running to help carry in groceries. Little Nathan was still sleeping soundly in his blanket wrap. We all hoped his treatment would bring him comfort and give his mother more rest that night.

"I don't think I'll stay up late this year," Clara said as she paid me five dollars for her trip. "Happy New Year to you!"

"Maybe I'll go buy some sauerkraut now, too," I replied, waving the five-dollar bill.

Back at the neighboring farm, Mr. Keim and the Schrock youth were taking church benches from a wagon to the house. Knowing how rushed everyone might be, I stopped to ask if they needed anything from town.

The mother of the bride motioned me inside from her rocking chair, where she was nursing her twelfth child. Long tables were already set up in three rooms with upside-down plates, glasses, and silverware in place for two hundred guests.

A teenage daughter was mixing batter, and I wondered if it was for the wedding cake.

"No, that's just for small loaf cakes to serve sliced at the meal," the mother replied. "Another neighbor is making a three-tier wedding cake, with roses on top. That's usually saved till last and cut for the attendants, cooks, and table waiters."

She couldn't think of anything they needed—except more time to get ready. When I turned to go, there beside the window was a long row of shoes —all sizes, men's and women's. And there with a stained cloth was a four-year-old girl, busily rubbing black polish all over them.

The Author

THE author's pen name is Jim Butterfield. He grew up near Holmes County, Ohio, the center of the largest Amish community in the world. With other town boys, he sometimes tried to hang onto the back springs and axle of Amish buggies coming into the county seat. One astute bearded driver offered him a ride in the buggy, and Jim has liked that horse-drawn pace ever since.

For several years he had his own folding-top rig (not used by the Amish), and one summer he worked on an Amish farm, driving draft teams. He likes the historic pattern of old-fashioned farming. He also worked with an Amish carpenter crew.

The author studied history at the College of Wooster and taught for two years in Amish areas of Holmes County. He drove for a rural bus line between Wooster and Millersburg, and sent a weekly column by "The Driver" to the Sugarcreek *Budget* about plain people and events along the route.

Jim wrote occasional articles for the local *Daily Record* newspaper while working for the City of Wooster and at Rubbermaid. He has also published articles in *The Holmes County Traveler*, *Northeast Ohio Avenues*, *Pennsylvania Dutchman* (now *Pennsylvania Folklife*), and the Cleveland *Plain Dealer*.

Butterfield sometimes guided tour buses into Holmes County. On one trip he met a teacher-passenger with a keen interest in the Amish—and married her in 1963. With their three children, they attended Kidron Mennonite Church.

Now retired, Jim remains on call to take Amish families for doctor appointments or to visit distant relatives. He belongs to the Unitarian-Universalist Fellowship of Wayne County and volunteers monthly at the Mennonite Information Center near Berlin, Ohio.

The author asks readers to notify the publisher of any mistakes or wrong impressions so that improvements can be made in any reprint.

The Photographer

THE photographer, Doyle Yoder, resides in Holmes County, Ohio. His pictures represent his native countryside and show the everyday life of the folks in Holmes County.

One buyer of his calendar told Yoder, "Your photos capture the land and the people. And you don't turn your subjects into cutesy curiosities like others do." As a result, Yoder enjoys wide acceptance and respect among the Amish people, not only in his own neighborhood but also in other Amish communities across United States and Canada.

Many of Yoder's photographs have been published in magazines and books throughout the country. His photos regularly grace covers of periodicals such as the *Holmes County Traveler, Country, Country Extra,* and *Reminisce*; and covers of books, brochures, and travel guides. In 1993 the American Travel Writers Foundation honored him with a silver medal for the best newspaper photo illustration of a travel article.

Yoder also collaborated with Les Kelly in producing *America's Amish Country*, a 136-page book with 313 color photographs featuring almost every Amish settlement in North America. He is actively involved with printers in the Holmes County area, doing photography and four-color prepress work. He also publishes postcards, note cards, and calendars. His address is given on the copyright page (page 4, above).

9963